Praise for *Beyond Grit for Business*

"Powerful, practical, and solid advice on high performance. Kamphoff's tools and insights will help you level up and trust yourself more. Share this with your people if you want to inspire a more motivated, responsible, and high-trust team!" **DAVID HORSAGER, CEO and bestselling author of *The Trust Edge***

"Keep this book close and refer to it often. It will be your go-to resource and either inspire or irritate you along your way. It will make the difference between performing well versus performing at your *best*—each and every day." **MARK LeBLANC, CSP, author of *Never Be the Same* and *Rainmaker Confidential***

"Grit is the breakfast of champions. With compassion and insight, and plenty of examples, Dr. Kamphoff shows us how to prepare it, cook it, and eat it so that it is easy to digest and fuels our ability to work through adversity, turn setbacks into comebacks, and continue on our desired path to success." **HENDRIE WEISINGER, PhD, author of the *New York Times* bestseller *Performing Under Pressure***

"Cindra is one of the world's leading experts when it comes to relating high performance along with the power of grit, and her newest book is a must-read for business executives, sales professionals, and entrepreneurs who want to succeed in the new economy." **ROSS BERNSTEIN, CSP, CPAE, inspirational business speaker**

"If you have *Beyond Grit for Business*, it's the one book you'll read again and again. Its information and strategies are priceless." **JEN TRUE, broker/owner, True Real Estate**

"Powerful, practical, and solid advice on high performance. Cindra Kamphoff's expertise will change the way you think about success at work." **GARY HOOGEVEEN, president and CEO, Rocky Mountain Power**

"Cindra gets it right when she says 'Believe the best is yet to come,' because if you read this book and apply these tools, your best performance is ahead of you." **ADAM J DeLAWYER, vice president at CHS, Inc.**

"I absolutely love *Beyond Grit for Business*. Every page is packed with golden insights and guidance to help readers bring the best they have to offer in work and life." **JIM AFREMOW, PhD, author of *The Champion's Mind***

"Dr. Cindra Kamphoff gets it right when she says 'Master Your Thoughts.' As someone who frequently has a lot of ideas but doesn't see them through, *Beyond Grit for Business* gave me actionable tools to get out of my own way and get s#!& done." **JAMES ROBILOTTA, professional speaker and author of *Leading Imperfectly***

"This book is a practical guide to achieving new performance horizons personally and professionally! Cindra is masterful at providing many small steps that, if applied consistently, could make a massive difference in your life and relationships!" **BJ HELLYER, managing director, Northwestern Mutual**

"Here is a powerhouse book of strategies, tools, and approaches to perform at your best that simply work. A fantastic book." **CHRISTINA BOHLKE, market president, BankVista Mankato**

"High Performers are always looking to get better. If you want to be better today than you were yesterday, then I would highly encourage you to read this book." **MICHAEL OLSEN, senior vice president - commercial sales, Consolidated Communications**

"Cindra Kamphoff's expertise will change the way you think about *you* and the value *you* bring to your organization. She shows that it is never too late to discover and unleash the valuable, powerful *you*." **SARAH RICHARDS, president, CEO, and board chair, Jones Metal, Inc.**

"*Beyond Grit for Business* makes so much sense. It takes the personal help book *Beyond Grit* to a new level by guiding entrepreneurs to business success with sage ethical and positive-thinking advice. Cindra gets 'it' and shares 'it' here." **JAY ABDO, retired senior partner, Abdo**

"*Beyond Grit for Business* is a *must-have* and *must-read* book. This book is filled with rich research, real stories, and practical applications that are designed to help you thrive in life, school, and work. I love Cindra Kamphoff's commitment and passion around helping people transform their lives, careers, and businesses utilizing the grit factor." **DR. JERMAINE M. DAVIS, award-winning professor of communication and organizational leadership**

"Cindra works with world-class athletes to improve their performance, and this book will take your business game to the next level. If you are looking for an edge, *Beyond Grit for Business* is your GPS to success." **JOE SCHMIT, speaker, author, broadcaster**

"If you want to go from the 'pity party' to your own personal 'launch party,' then this is the book for you. Cindra has filled this book with techniques that help you turn stress into fuel. If you don't read this book, your business will fail miserably." **JIM YOUNG, senior VP and regional manager, Edina Realty Homeservices**

"Anyone who's ever wanted to get to the next level or help their team elevate will absolutely love the practical tools in this book. It's a must-read! And if you lead a team, it's a perfect book for all your employees." **KRISTEN BROWN, energy mastery expert and bestselling author**

"Wow, what a great book that Cindra has put together for business owners! As soon as I started to read it, I knew I needed to take notes so I could apply many of the practices in my businesses. I started today with the 'Seven-Day Challenge.' This book is a manual for success. The 10 Practices are very powerful ways that a business owner can lead themselves and their teams to greatness." **MIKE HAMEL, owner of Hamel Coaching and Consulting and of HMA Paving and Contracting Corp.**

"I have been learning from Cindra for a number of years. Cindra's teachings are concise, compelling, and immediately applicable to any professional regardless of success level. The principles in *Beyond Grit for Business* are timeless and will help you level up your career as they have for my business." **DAN HAGER, managing director, Northwestern Mutual**

"*Beyond Grit for Business* is perfect given all of the change we are facing in business today. The book teaches great lessons and provides powerful ways for application. This is a roadmap to tackling tough changes and to implementing innovation in your business." **JOE S. NAYQUONABE, CEO of Mille Lacs Corporate Ventures**

"Whether you're an aspiring entrepreneur, a seasoned business owner, or a business executive, *Beyond Grit for Business* cuts through to the core concepts that push high performers to greater achievement. Cindra's Top 10 Practices are invaluable tools to level up high performance and achieve your potential to navigate today's complex business environment." **BRENDAN MOORE, architecture, engineering, and construction industry executive**

"Cindra has done it again. This is a must-read for anyone who wants to level up!" **TIM McNIFF, Emmy Award-winning news and sports anchor and entrepreneur**

"Here is a powerhouse book of strategies, tools, and approaches to perform at your best that simply work. What a practical and easy book to read! These strategies have helped me and my employees perform at our best." **TROY D. KALIS, EVP/chief retail lending officer, Frandsen Bank & Trust**

"Cindra's Top 10 Practices of the World's Best are principles that dramatically enhance performance as a leader, entrepreneur, or salesperson. If you are looking at taking yourself, your team, and your business to the next level, this book is a *must* to help you get there." **PAM SOLBERG-TAPPER, MHSA, PCC, BCC, executive coach, speaker, 7 Continents Marathoner, owner of Coach for Success, Inc.**

"Cindra Kamphoff's expertise will change the way you think about your self-image. She has changed the way we communicate with employees, coworkers, and business partners. This book is a must-read!" **AVI AND ETHAN DERHY, fourth-generation small business owners, Signal Garage Auto Care**

"This must-read guide for leaders, salespeople, and entrepreneurs contains everything you need to know if you want to achieve high performance." **ANGELA COX, Midwest Speakers Bureau, Inc.**

"Cindra has nailed it once again! Reading this and embodying the Beyond Grit mindset is a game-changer for anyone! Why? Because when you blow past the limitations of your mind, you become unstoppable." **JANE ATKINSON, author, *The Wealthy Speaker 2.0***

"This book is a must-read if you have a nagging sensation that there's more to life and business than what you're currently experiencing. *Beyond Grit for Business* is a masterclass on self-leadership that will help you break through the barriers to high performance, reach your true potential, and fulfill your life's purpose." **JON LOKHORST, leadership coach, speaker, trainer, and author of *Mission-Critical Leadership: How Smart Managers Lead Well in All Directions***

"There is a saying that goes like this: 'A good story beats data every day.' That might be true, but what if you had good stories and good data? *Beyond Grit for Business* uses stories masterfully; provides ten practical, feasible, and implementable performance practices; and backs it all up with data! I highly recommend this book for individuals, especially those in leadership roles, who want to be high performers. It's a fun read!" **JOHN B. MOLIDOR, PhD, CSP, CEO, president of Brain-Based Leadership Institute and past president of the National Speakers Association**

"Dr. Kamphoff introduces mindset changes in bite-size pieces that are easy and practical to turn into sustainable habits. Her ideas and tools are transformative. More than a book, this is a go-to life guide!" **RON VETTER, CEO and chairman, Vetter Stone and Alabama Stone**

BEYOND GRIT FOR BUSINESS

TEN POWERFUL PRACTICES TO BOOST PERFORMANCE, LEADERSHIP, AND YOUR BOTTOM LINE

Cindra Kamphoff, Ph.D.

ISBN 13: 978-1-63489-532-3

Library of Congress Catalog Number has been applied for.
Printed in the United States of America
First Printing: 2022

26 25 24 23 22 5 4 3 2 1

Cover design by Nupoor Gordon
Interior design by Cindy Samargia Laun and Dan Pitts

Wise Ink Creative Publishing
807 Broadway St NE
Suite 46
Minneapolis, MN 55413

To my parents, Hank and Bev,
who first taught me about the mindset
of an entrepreneur.

Contents

Foreword

When Cindra asked me to consider writing the foreword to her new book, I was terrified. Don't get me wrong; I was excited and flattered that she thought I could offer something relevant. And as the founder of Angie's BOOMCHICKAPOP, I've told my story thousands of times through speaking events, podcasts, and interviews. So what was I fretting about? I'm not an author (sigh), but if *she* thought I had the grit and courage, who was I to disagree? (*Take a step back from your anxiety, Angie, and just start writing!*) Dr. Cindra Kamphoff is an expert at distilling the complicated nuances that create high-level performers and leaders in both business and sports. And you'll want to absorb every bit of wisdom in this book.

I'm not exactly sure when I first met Cindra, but I know it was before we sold BOOMCHICKAPOP. I'd begun to hear a buzz in our community about a talented young PhD who was the director of the Center for Sport and Performance Psychology at Minnesota State University, Mankato. When I first heard her speak on performance, it was in the context of sports. Her style and the content immediately resonated with me. First, I thought, *The children in my life need to hear this!* On the way to my car, I called coaches and athletic directors, explaining why they needed to get Dr. Kamphoff to talk to our kids. (Yes, I'm one of *those* parents . . . but in a good way.) The coaches were already on it; I hadn't been the only parent to make the request. Secondly, and coincidentally, Cindra had basically described my experiences and my husband

Dan's experiences as entrepreneurs—practices we knew were spot on but hadn't taken the time to articulate. Apparently, we'd been doing all that gritty "sports stuff" (my words, not hers) all along while building Angie's BOOMCHICKAPOP.

Back when we started popping popcorn in our single-car garage, Dan was a teacher, a father, and a baseball coach, and I was a working mom, a volunteer, and a psychiatric nurse practitioner. Our children were three and five years old. We were happy with our lives, but we were also a little restless, believing there was more we could do together as a family. We were teaching our children the value of work along with the goal of putting some money away for their college fund. That purpose evolved over time. We wanted our business to have integrity and be something that made us and our community proud. We wanted our employees to be the best versions of themselves and to feel welcome, and we wanted to create a work community that felt like family.

When we bought a ten-by-ten-foot tent and an outdoor kettle, we didn't imagine what our little side hustle would become—especially not that it would sell to Conagra Brands sixteen years later for a quarter of a billion dollars. We loaded the equipment into and out of our Ford Explorer until we could afford a trailer. We sold three-dollar and five-dollar bags of kettle corn at college and amateur sporting events, on street corners, in front of grocery and big-box stores, at neighborhood festivals, and at Minnesota Vikings home games.

We thought that if we could sell kettle corn at the Minnesota State Fair, that would be proof we'd made it. But the State Fair turned us down. We had to live and let go. If we had held on to that definition of success, we would have called ourselves failures. Instead, we redefined our goal. If that failure had not happened, Dan and I would probably still be hauling our equipment to the Minnesota State Fairgrounds every August in the Midwest heat, and there would never have been an Angie's BOOMCHICKAPOP, nor would we have been able to share the success with our hundreds of employees, our investment partners, and our community.

Along the way, we learned how to get comfortable in uncomfortable situations (Practice 10: Choose Your Courage Zone). We had to channel energy, persist through our anxiety, problem-solve quickly, ask for help, and use everything in our lives to create something of worth (Practice 7: Choose Empowering Emotions). Even our tiniest successes confirmed that we were on the right track. Our critics and competitors were our greatest motivators. We learned how to change, adjust, and evolve the business. We didn't get stuck or wallow in our failures—but instead used them as fertilizer to grow our business, focusing on what we could control (Practice 9: Live and Let Go).

Popcorn wasn't necessarily our passion, but making simple, healthier food absolutely was. Transparency in labeling, sharing our success, believing in people's goodness, and creating empowered lives—these were (and still are) our passions. This meant creating a safe work environment, not just by OSHA's standards. We thought about employee safety as being both physical and emotional, the latter of which Cindra refers to as *psychological safety* in Practice 9. For us, psychological safety was about creating a culture where people felt liberated to bring their authentic selves, ideas, perspectives, and life experiences into the workplace. People are more likely to unleash their creative energy when they feel safe and free to be their authentic selves. Problem-solving and ideating from diverse angles gave us an advantage in the marketplace as our team worked together toward a common goal—paradoxically making and selling popcorn.

We listened to the people that were buying our popcorn. Dan's cell phone number was our business line, and it was printed on every bag of popcorn for the first ten years. (I know, I know . . .

there are other ways. We didn't change the practice until we could afford to hire customer service representatives.) When he answered the phone, it might have been a trucker looking for a dock time, a consumer complaining that our popcorn wasn't salty enough, or a mother standing and reading our ingredient label at the grocery store, wanting to know if the popcorn is "certified gluten-free." This helped create an intimate connection with the people buying our products. We learned what mattered to them. We answered their questions. We sought certifications that made some of their lives a little easier when buying groceries.

We also listened to ourselves. I did not want artificial ingredients or preservatives in our popcorn, which meant that the ingredients we desired were both harder to find and more expensive. I saw pristine ingredients and packaging as investments. But to the operations and finance departments, it was "a hit to the margin." Both were true. You find a way to choose; it is all about priorities.

When Cindra and I had a chance to connect a few years later, she had a thriving business working with executives, businesses, and high-performing athletes. She was not only teaching and coaching—she was *doing*! I was invited to tell our story and reflect on the Angie's BOOMCHICKAPOP journey on her *High Performance Mindset* podcast in 2016. Cindra asked the question, "Did you have a defining or 'aha' moment?" Life is full of those moments, big and small. It's rich with learning and growth for the willing. Whether it's the result of inspiration or necessity, I've learned that everything I've done until this moment created what I needed for this moment. It's possible to do the things that scare you, and when you do, you grow. You can find your courage every day. I'm Angie Bastian, cofounder of Angie's BOOMCHICKAPOP, and I'm finding it today. Now it's your turn!

Angie Bastian

Introduction

On one of the final days of my senior year of high school, I ran the fastest mile in the state of Iowa for the year. It was one of the best days of my life. I had reached my potential, experienced flow, and accomplished a goal I had worked to accomplish daily for two years.

4:46.68—that was my finishing time, and it's still cemented in my brain some twenty-five years later. I had won the state championship. As I stood on the top of the podium in the middle of the field, there was so much promise for me. A talented, gritty, passionate runner who had dreams of being an all-American in college and, someday, an Olympian. I had the talent and the work ethic to make it happen—but not the mindset skills.

My performances that year earned me a full scholarship at the University of Northern Iowa, where I would run on the cross-country and track teams. I was proud to be in the highest division of college athletics, and I couldn't wait to show what I had inside me. As a fiery and gritty runner, my freshman and sophomore years in college showed a lot of promise. I came in second on my team in most races. My grit and work ethic was paying off.

That summer, between my sophomore and junior years, I doubled down on my training; I moved to Santa Fe, New Mexico, to train and live with my sister and brother-in-law. I came back more fit and ready to compete. People told me, "Wow, Cindra, this will be *your* year!" At the time, I believed it *would* be my year. After a second-place finish behind an all-American (the title I was going after) named Sydney Pounds, I was on a natural high. *Yes, this* is *my year! All my training is paying off. I could become an all-American. I just raced alongside one.*

The next week, my team competed in Minneapolis in one of the biggest meets of the season. I started off neck and neck with the all-Americans, then suddenly, out of nowhere, the doubt crept in. *You don't deserve to run with these runners, Cindra. You're nothing like them. You're not fast enough. You're not fit enough. You're not enough. You're not enough. You're not . . .* I listened to that pounding voice inside my head, believing every word. And as I listened, I ran slower and slower . . . eventually dropping out of the race. I had just finished second the week before! I felt like an embarrassment. I had disappointed my team, my parents, and—most importantly—myself. My confidence plummeted that day (after one race), and I never recovered during my last two years on the team. I didn't know how to get out of my own way. I let one poor performance shatter my confidence and my passion.

I have regrets about that time in my life. Deep down, I know I didn't reach my potential. I kept getting in my own way. I was not mentally strong. I didn't know *how* to be mentally strong. I didn't have the tools and strategies to grow my mindset. I felt like a head case, and I thought my teammates thought the same about me. I had a lot of potential and grit, but I couldn't put it together when it mattered because I kept listening to and believing the lies my mind kept telling me.

Looking back now, I know this difficulty happened *for* me, not *to* me. It was a gift because it led me to this incredible work on mindset. I have a deep passion for this work because I don't want *anyone* to feel like I did—as if they left their potential somewhere and kept getting in their own way, their confidence shattered by one bad day or poor performance. That's a yucky, nasty feeling in your gut, and it can feel like torture. I also know this difficulty was a gift because it led me to earn a PhD in sport and performance psychology, which ultimately helped me understand myself but also taught me the practices, strategies, and mental tools that are used by the World's Best and that form the basis of this book.

After earning my PhD, I started my career as a college professor, writing, teaching, and researching performance psychology. I loved mentoring the next generation of mental-performance practitioners (and still do it today), but something was missing. Was I really "going for it," or was I just playing it safe? On April 15, 2013, I finally understood what was missing.

I had gotten back into running and competing—this time for the love and passion of it, not for the titles or accolades that had driven my motivation during my junior and senior years of college. I had just finished my third Boston Marathon, my tenth overall marathon. And I'd crushed it! It felt like my senior year of high school all over again. I had pushed myself mentally and physically to run the race of a lifetime. I saw the impact that mastering my mindset had on my performance and happiness. I felt free. Proud, full of adrenaline, and happy with my performance, I walked back to my hotel. Then, suddenly, the race didn't matter.

After I heard the news—that a terrorist bombing at the finish line had killed three people and injured an estimated 264 others, including fourteen who required amputations—I sat quietly in my hotel room, near the finish line, scared out of my mind. I could see the finish line from my window. As I watched news reports on the terrorist attack and the manhunt that followed, I tried to make sense of it all. *I could have been killed. Why was I spared, but so many others were injured or even killed?*

Then I asked myself three pivotal questions that changed my life:

- Why am I here?

- What difference am I making in this world?

- Why do I do what I do?

That day was a turning point in my life. Afterward, I started making different decisions about my time, energy, and focus. I began a journey to understand my calling, my purpose, and my uniqueness. I started doing the hard work (still doing it today)— reading, learning, and exploring. I felt in my soul that I had to find my calling, because life could end any moment. I started to practice more regularly what I had learned in graduate school and in the time since. That led me to start my own business, which has exploded since then, providing ample opportunities for me to share my wisdom, knowledge, and experiences. Once I'd embraced my calling and purpose, I began choosing courage and doing something scary each day (more on this later), which has had a positive impact on my life as well as the lives of others.

Asking myself, *How can I follow my purpose today and do something uncomfortable?* led me to work with professional athletes—including working one-on-one with Olympians as well as Minnesota Vikings players. Along the way, I found professional speaking and began to speak more and more around the country, teaching businesses and teams about mindset and grit. As I delivered keynotes and trainings, more and more executives, leaders, and salespeople were asking if I would coach them like I did professional athletes.

What gives me energy? is a question I ask myself weekly. I use it to help me determine if I should say yes or say no to opportunities in pursuit of living my passion and calling. I've found that working with an entrepreneur, salesperson, or business leader gives me the same energy as working one-on-one with a professional athlete. And that's why I wrote this book—for you. Just as a professional athlete trains their mind to make sound decisions on their trek to the podium, you must train your mind to make sound decisions on your trek to achieving your big business vision. It's too easy to get in your own way and limit your potential—I know this from experience—and I was put on the Earth to help you master the inner game of business so you can reach your potential.

I, too, have gotten in my own way as an entrepreneur. I stopped writing my first book for six months, wondering if anyone would read it. When I first started keynoting, I struggled with showing up as my authentic self onstage, and I questioned if I should (or even could) charge the same fee as my male colleagues. To be honest, I still get in my own way from time to time. But implementing the practices in this book allows me to get unstuck quicker, lead more effectively, and build my business toward my bold vision.

Now, as an executive and performance coach, I see the ways that entrepreneurs, executives, salespeople, and business leaders get in their own way. They share with me their deepest disempowering beliefs and harsh, damaging self-talk. The executives, managers, and CEOs who look like they have it all together are often the ones who reveal a different story behind closed doors. Behind the facade of control and confidence, many of them experience fear, don't feel worthy of their success, and/or believe they're not good enough—just like the rest of us can. It's shocking how hard we can be on ourselves, the things we can say. In my coaching relationships, I have my clients work to move forward with more empowering beliefs and powerful self-talk, which helps them lead more authentically, take risks toward their courageous vision, and live more purposefully.

I love helping others on this journey to overcome their limiting beliefs, develop their leadership skills, realize their purpose, and live a bigger vision for themselves. This work helps entrepreneurs, business leaders, and salespeople believe that *any* vision is possible to build and that *they* can build it. Yes, *any* vision is possible for *you* to build! Any dream is possible with enough daily focus, belief in your vision, and awareness of self. Any destiny you want, you can have. And yes, *you* can build it!

Working with top athletes at the professional level has taught me the importance of capitalizing on your talents and skills. But talent and skill alone are not enough to allow you to step into your potential. I've seen too many athletes come into the NFL with talent and skill—only to get cut from the team because their mindset isn't in the right place. They focus on the outcome, fearing they will get cut, or the pressure ends up being too much to handle. They don't achieve their dream or vision because they got in their own way mentally.

And that is why I wrote this book specifically for *you*—the executive, entrepreneur, salesperson, and/or business leader. My hope for you after reading this book is that you'll feel more confident reaching for the financial goals you've secretly been too afraid to shoot for, that you'll feel as capable internally as you project to your colleagues externally, and that, finally, you'll have the tools to overcome the next roadblock that threatens to throw you off your game. To me, that's what life is all about!

WHY I WROTE THIS BOOK

Mindset is contagious. When you adopt the mindset of a high performer, others around you will too. As a leader, you are (1) leading yourself and (2) leading others toward a common goal or purpose. However, most leaders skip right to leading others. Rule #1: You will not be effective at leading others until you're first effective at leading yourself. Your mindset impacts everything—from your communication style, to your mood, to your ability to inspire and activate a plan. Part of building the business you desire involves problem-solving. Any problem in a business starts with the psychology of the person leading that business. As a leader, it is important that you think and act like a high performer, because your team is watching, observing how you think, act, and solve problems. When you lead yourself first, you can lead others more powerfully.

Leading yourself, or *self-leadership*, is a foundational part of effectively leading others. Defined by Ana Lucia Kazan and Andrew Bryant, *self-leadership* is "the practice of intentionally influencing your thinking, feeling and actions toward your objective(s)." When you master self-leadership, you're more innovative, fearless, positive, and healthy. If you can make self-leadership a priority, you will experience less stress and access greater fulfillment.

Your mindset impacts your relationships, your leadership, and, ultimately, your career. Your mindset powers everything about you—your thoughts, beliefs, feelings, and actions—as well as the business that you will or won't build, the vision that you will or won't realize. *You* get to decide.

You may think that mental conditioning is like riding a bike—that once you learn it, you can always do it—but that's not the case. The best of the best know that mastering mindset requires daily effort and practice; if you take a day off, your business, life, and performance suffer. And that's why I am pumped you are reading this book to help you train your mindset and reach your ultimate potential.

YOUR POTENTIAL

One of the objectives of this book is to help you reach your potential. In fact, I define *high performance* as "a purposeful, daily pursuit of excellence and your potential." You may be wondering, *What exactly is my potential?* Potential is unlimited. It is endless. Just when you feel as if you've reached your potential, you know you are capable of more. Discovering your potential is about the following:

- Your commitment to being your best self and uncovering the limiting beliefs, assumptions, and negativity that can get in your way.

- Connecting with your authentic self, not acting like someone else.

- Looking deep inside yourself, not seeking other people's approval.

- Getting clarity on what you really want and why.

- Ultimately, using the ten practices in this book.

Given that potential is limitless, consider the question, *What is getting in the way of your unlimited potential?* It may be a lack of clear direction, not taking enough action, or doing or believing something that isn't working over and over again. Or maybe your limiting beliefs—that you can't make a change, aren't good enough, or aren't smart enough—are getting in your way, as mine did several years ago in college.

Now consider the question, *What would your life look like at the next level, once you have realized your potential?* However you answer that question—however you see it in your mind—gives you a good glimpse of your potential. Maybe you are seeking more fulfillment, consistent happiness, or a stronger ability and determination to go after your goals. Great athletes visualize results before they happen. You, too, can visualize your life and business at the next level to connect with your potential. And I can't wait to hear about how you connect with your potential as a result of reading this book!

HOW TO USE THIS BOOK

Beyond Grit for Business is organized around ten practices that represent the psychological practices of the best leaders, executives, entrepreneurs, and salespeople. These ten practices lead to greatness, realization of potential, and consistent high performance, and they will help you build the business of your dreams—that is, *if* you apply and practice them. These practices are supported by scientific research on business, performance psychology, positive psychology, and neuroscience.

In the original *Beyond Grit*, I outlined all ten practices in a comprehensive way. In this book, however, I break down the ten practices and apply them specifically to you—the entrepreneur, executive, salesperson, and/or business leader. The small changes you make as you read this book will have a big impact in building the business of your dreams. Tiny shifts can bring massive change. We'll start by getting gritty, but you'll need the other nine practices to truly get where you want and build the business you desire. It's going *beyond* grit that leads to mastering your mindset and reaching your potential, to realizing your bold vision and building the business of your dreams. And you must practice each of the ten practices *daily* to get to where you want to go.

Top 10 Practices of the World's Best

1. The World's Best
   are gritty.

2. The World's Best
   are clear on their purpose.

3. The World's Best
   are masters of their thoughts.

4. The World's Best
   know themselves to master themselves.

5. The World's Best
   dominate the controllables.

6. The World's Best
   own the moment.

7. The World's Best
   choose empowering emotions.

8. The World's Best
   own who they are.

9. The World's Best
   live and let go.

10. The World's Best
    choose their courage zone.

As you read, focus on the *how*, because the *how* is the secret sauce. As humans, we tend to get in our own way, and we need tangible, actionable ways to build our mindset and live the ten practices to reach our potential. That's the focus of this book—showing you *how* to implement the ten practices, because that is what will have the biggest impact on your life and business. Knowing doesn't create change; it's the doing that creates change. Knowledge isn't power; implementation is power. You may know everything discussed in this book, but you *must* put it into action to see the results. It's great to understand these ten principles, but using them on a daily basis is the game changer.

Your mindset is your engine, powering everything you do. Powering your engine with high-octane strategies and tools is key.

You must power your mind with high-octane strategies and tools to have the impact you desire—and you must do it daily. And if you need accountability and direction to implement these ten practices, check out my coaching group, available at cindrakamphoff.com.

HOW THIS BOOK WILL BENEFIT YOU

Since the original *Beyond Grit* was published, I have heard from people all over the world about the impact the book has had on building their businesses, for which I am incredibly grateful. Below I share a few examples to help you understand the impact of what you are reading and the power of shifting your mindset to the practices outlined in this book:

- I met Kelly at an Optimist Club meeting at which I was speaking. Shortly after our paths crossed, she said goodbye to corporate America to start her own marketing business, which was thriving just a year later. She said, "This guidebook gave me the courage and the oomph to start my own business. Its practical advice was a game changer for me to have the confidence to build the business of my dreams."

- Leo, a financial planner, desired to take his business to the next level. He specifically wanted more time pursuing his dream clients. He said, "The *Beyond Grit* practices made all the difference. [They] led me to my best year in terms of revenue! I am now more deliberate and focused with my time, and clearly see where I am going and how to get there. I am realizing my potential."

- Amy, the CEO of a manufacturing company, said that the ten practices helped her navigate through change: "If it weren't for this work on my mindset, I would have had to take my personal money to fund the business. Instead, I had the courage to make a change in personnel that would drastically change our trajectory. We grew by 30 percent that year because of it."

- Adam, an entrepreneur, decided he wanted to start his own coaching practice, where he would support others in building their own businesses. He said, "The ten practices helped me take massive action and choose courage to market my business and share my message. I've now launched my business and attracted my first clients, which is helping me live my purpose and find my potential."

Those stories and many more like them are why I am so excited to share this book with you! I want you to have the tools you need to get clarity on your vision, understand your purpose, and overcome limiting beliefs to help you take bold, massive action.

APPLYING THIS BOOK

This book focuses on ten practices to add to your High Performance Toolbox to help you take massive action toward your bold vision. Each chapter (one practice each) will help you uncover how to shift your mindset with one of the *Beyond Grit* practices. Each chapter also ends with a High Performance Game Plan to help you implement the practice as well as a Power Phrase to help you develop the High Performance Mindset. As you become acquainted with each of the practices, write a Power Phrase on a notecard or on your mirror (with a dry-erase marker) to make it a focus for your day or week. I also offer *Beyond Grit* cards, each highlighting a Power Phrase that you can use to guide your actions each day, available at cindrakamphoff. com.

All of the exercises and tools are important in this book, but there is one exercise that is a complete life and game changer. Starting each day with the GRIT Morning Routine and Priming Exercise is a must! Spend a few minutes before you dive into the first practice reflecting on how you can start your morning with energy, passion, and courage to discover your potential and the vision that you desire.

Alternate Ways to Read This Book (Optional)

Beyond Grit for Business is a bit more focused than the original *Beyond Grit*, and if the approach I presented on the previous page works for you, *great!* However, if you're a fan of the first book, or if you just like options, consider the following (updated) ways to read this book:

High Performance Level 1
Read and Learn

- Read this book and learn the practices and tools needed to improve your life and build the business you desire.

- While still valuable, this level would have the lowest impact.

High Performance Level 2
Apply and Do

- Take the practices and tools presented and implement them in your life and business.

- This level would have a moderate impact.

High Performance Level 3
Live and Teach

- Live the principles of the World's Best and teach others how to adopt the High Performance Mindset, which facilitates consistent performance and a business that flourishes, not to mention leads to happiness, fulfillment, and a life on your terms.

- This level would have the most impact.

GRIT MORNING ROUTINE AND PRIMING EXERCISE

People ask me all the time, "How do *you* train your mind, Cindra?" One of the ways I choose to feel good first thing in the morning is with a simple morning routine that primes me to have a great day. The GRIT Morning Routine is a psychological jumpstart to your day.

Most people don't have a compelling reason to jump out of bed in the morning. They would rather sleep a little longer, feeling overwhelmed by the priorities and to-dos of the day. Or, they might pick up their phone, check their email, or browse social media as they continue to lie in bed. Doing that can make you feel overwhelmed by other people's priorities or the negativity of the world instead of priming yourself to have a great day.

The three most important reasons you want to start your day with the GRIT Morning Routine are:

1. You are intentionally choosing your morning focus.

2. You are jumpstarting your day by choosing empowering emotions.

3. By doing so habitually, you are developing the mindset and neurotransmitters needed to thrive and discover your potential.

Many of my clients tell me that when they start their day with the GRIT Morning Routine, the focus and emotions they choose help them lead more intentionally and authentically, and they are more motivated, happy, and patient throughout their day.

Tom, an owner of multiple auto shops with combined annual sales over $10 million, told me that after he primed his focus with gratitude for his employees one morning, he was able to show more compassion when one employee was getting under his skin later in the day. In the past, he would have become angry or frustrated, but priming helped him intentionally choose the way he wanted to respond. The focus and emotions you *choose* in the morning will shape your day and your ability to respond (not react) to challenges head-on. By following the GRIT Morning Routine every day, you are strengthening the neural pathways associated with choosing empowering emotions.

Many of the World's Best leaders have discussed how morning routines have shaped their leadership. Arianna Huffington, the cofounder and editor in chief of the *Huffington Post*, has a regular morning routine that includes many of the GRIT Morning Routine components. In *My Morning Routine*, she said, "A big part of my morning ritual is about what I don't do: when I wake up, I don't start the day by looking at my smartphone. Instead, once I'm awake, I take a minute to breathe deeply, be grateful, and set my intention for the day."

Priming in the morning allows you to start your day on fire, with lasting impact. Although best done in the morning, priming can also be used to reset after a setback during your day. You could pair the GRIT Priming Exercise with physical exercise in the morning or include it as part of your meditation or morning ritual.

The four components of the exercise include some of my best tools to help you create a business and life that align with your calling and ignite your gifts and potential. These tools will help you combat burnout and lift you out of moments of panic, self-doubt, and wheel-spinning negativity.

As part of the exercise, I recommend you *spend at least one minute with each component*, but there is no maximum time. On an hour run, for example, I often focus on the GRIT Priming Exercise for the whole hour. When I do, I am on fire, with creative ideas flowing. The impact on my day, my business, and my life is unreal!

You'll find the GRIT Priming Exercise below:

> **GRIT Priming Exercise**
>
> - G: Gratitude for Everything
>
> - R: Remember Your *Why* or Purpose
>
> - I: Intentions (State at Least 3)
>
> - T: Talk to Yourself with Your Power Phrases

G:

Gratitude for Everything – Like a highlight reel, think about the relationships, life experiences, business opportunities, and even the difficulties you are grateful for. Big moments or small moments, great moments or difficult moments—consider them all.

R:

Remember Your *Why* or Purpose – Consider your answers to the prompt "I do what I do so that . . ." either in your mind or out loud. You could also use your answers to the *ikigai* exercise in chapter 2 (page 55) or the Purpose Statement Exercise in the original *Beyond Grit* book to guide thinking about your purpose. Then visualize the people you will impact today by living your purpose statement through your actions. Consider the ripple effects that living your purpose will create. How will you show up today to live your purpose and serve others? As you will learn in chapter 2, living a life of service creates the highest level of momentum.

I:

Intentions – State three intentions for the day, either in your mind or out loud. Your intentions should take the form of "I will . . ." statements. Consider more "be" intentions instead of "do" intentions, though both are powerful. In other words, focus more on how you want to show up and less on the task(s) you want to complete. Who do you want to be today? How do you want to show up with courage and purpose, doing at least one thing that is uncomfortable? Imagine how your day will go based on your intentions. Think about ways you will be kind to yourself, courageously moving toward your bold vision, or reward yourself throughout the day by pausing, breathing, and practicing compassion for others and for yourself. Here are some examples of daily intentions:

- "I will boldly lead my team today."

- "I will be compassionate while giving my employee feedback."

- "I will be fully present during my meetings."

- "I will act with courage, remembering that my business changes lives."

- "I will do one thing that is uncomfortable today."

- "I will pause when I feel frustrated and take a breath to refocus."

T:

Talk to Yourself with Your Power Phrases – The last step is to state 10–30 Power Phrases in your mind or out loud with passion, confidence, and certainty—with grit! You should feel your Power Phrases in your body. A Power Phrase is a powerful statement that reflects how you want to condition yourself to think. If these statements don't come naturally, try asking yourself these questions: *What do I need to believe about myself, my leadership, and my ability to reach my vision for myself and my business? To level up my business, what do I need to believe about my value or the value my business provides?* You should be able to turn your answers into Power Phrases with little trouble. I have found that writing your Power Phrases out and repeating them each morning helps you become all you want to become and serve those you are intended to serve. Repeating your Power Phrases each morning will create change within you. You will learn more about Power Phrases in chapter 3. For now, you can use the following prompts to start your Power Phrases:

- "I am . . ."

- "Every day and in every way, I am . . ."

- "I take . . ."

- "I learn . . ."

- "I know . . ."

- "I show . . ."

- "Every day, I . . ."

(You can download a one-page PDF of the Grit Priming Exercise at beyondgrit.com/morning.)

To give you an example and help this exercise come alive, here is my GRIT Morning Routine from this morning:

G: Gratitude for Everything – "I am grateful for my supportive and loving husband, Dan, and my two boys, Carter and Blake. They are the reason I am here. I am grateful for a warm home to live in during a cold winter day in Minnesota. Even though it was tough, I am grateful for the difficult moment I had yesterday, when my internal judge got activated, and I was short with a colleague. It reminded me of how I don't want to act."

R: Remember Your *Why* or Purpose – I stated my purpose with energy and fire, reminding me why I am here: "The purpose of my life is to be connected and inspired, to guide others through wisdom and truth, helping them to play and live fully." I visualized the way I would live my purpose today through my writing, impacting you positively as you read this chapter.

I: Intentions – *Who do I want to be today?* I asked myself. My answer: "I will write in an inspiring way, connected to my best self and my heart. I will be kind, loving, and patient with my family. I will be kind to myself when I feel judged, frustrated, or angry." Then I visualized myself acting and showing up in those ways.

T: Talk to Yourself with Your Power Phrases – I stated my 30 Power Phrases (I have them written down) out loud with energy and passion. Here are some of my Power Phrases:

- "I know my value and the value of my work."

- "The tools I teach change people's lives."

- "I am love."

- "I am grace."

- "I am perfect just the way I am."

- "I am a thought leader."

- "I am a force for good."

- "I am a pioneer who gives her life to serving others."

- "I am one of the best damn keynote speakers people have heard."

- "I show my radiant energy."

- "I shine."

- "My work is important to this world."

- "Every day, I learn as if my actions change a million lives."

- "People I meet help me grow."

- "I take bold action."

- "I show grace with myself and others daily."

- "I step into my destiny."

- "All I need is within me now."

Before we dive into the ten practices, remember this: You were made to dream big dreams. You were put on the Earth to reach your potential. You were made to be gritty and stay gritty! You are reading this book because you were made for something more. You were made to build your business toward your bold vision, to dream for a living. You deserve anything you desire. Yes, it will take hard work, deliberate focus, and mastering your mind *every single day*. But remember: you can't take a day off of training your mind. You have all the resources you need inside you. It's time to turn them on. Let's go!

ADDITIONAL RESOURCES

It would mean the world to me to hear from you about what practices or tools made the most impact for you in building the business and life you desire and deserve.

You can contact me via the following:

- Email – cindra@cindrakamphoff.com

- Twitter – @Mentally_Strong

- LinkedIn – linkedin.com/in/cindra-kamphoff

- Instagram – @cindrakamphoff

- Facebook – @drcindrakamphoff

As you make this journey to conditioning your mindset as a leader, you may find other resources helpful. If you need accountability and support, you can sign up for our coaching group at cindrakamphoff.com. Additional resources are available at beyondgrit.com/bonus, including the following:

- "GRIT Priming Exercise" PDF

- Grit Values exercise

- "Connecting with Your Potential" meditation

- Video examples of Power Phrases

- And more . . .

We also have other resources to help you keep mastering your mindset daily—Beyond Grit Workbook, Beyond Grit Power Phrase Cards, motivational T-shirts, etc.—available at CindraKamphoff.com.

Get Gritty

The World's Best
know what they want and
they know why they want it.
In the face of adversity and setbacks,
they go after their goals with
deep commitment.

Chapter 1

Get Gritty

> "Everybody has their own Mount Everest—
> we were put on this earth to climb."
> —SETH GODIN, ENTREPRENEUR AND AUTHOR

After dreaming of being a trial attorney but failing her LSAT twice, Sara Blakely found herself selling fax machines door-to-door (it was the '90s). In 1998, while she was getting ready for a party, she decided to cut the feet off her pantyhose and wear them under her new cream slacks. "This allowed me to benefit from the slimming effects of the pantyhose's 'control top' while allowing my feet to go bare in my cute sandals," she said in *Getting There: A Book of Mentors*. "The moment I saw how good my butt looked, I was like, 'Thank you, God, this is my opportunity!'" The idea for Spanx was born that day, and the undergarment company now has over one hundred employees and pulls in $250 million in annual revenue.

She said that while selling fax machines, she would spend much of her time trying to figure out what she wanted to do with her life and where her strengths lay. "I knew I was good at selling and that I eventually wanted to be self-employed," she recalled. "I thought, *Instead of fax machines, I'd love to sell something that I created and actually care about*." She set that intention two years before the idea for Spanx came to her the night of that party.

Sara started Spanx with $5,000 of her own money. She hustled hard for many years before finally selling her first product to Neiman Marcus by asking the product manager if she would come to the bathroom and see the before and after on Sara, wearing the same pair of white slacks. Obviously, that sealed the deal, and the retailer put the product in seven stores to begin with. Sara spent hours and hours in the Neiman Marcus stores. She said, "I went to the stores, and I would explain what the product was. I would demo it. I'd show the before and after picture that my friend took. And then I would stand in the store from 9:00, when they opened, until about 5:00 or 6:00 every day." She would even ask her friends to buy her product and then reimburse them. "I needed to do whatever I could to maximize this chance," she explained.

Five years of hustle later, Sara landed on the cover of *Forbes Magazine* for being the youngest self-made female billionaire in the world. In the interview, she said her biggest piece of advice for entrepreneurs is to differentiate themselves and to understand what their customers need. She is widely quoted for saying, "Don't be intimidated by what you don't know. That can be your greatest strength and ensure that you do things differently from everyone else." She also credits much of her success to her father, who regularly asked, at the dinner table, "What did you guys fail at this week?" Sara said, "If we had nothing to tell him, he'd be disappointed. He knew that many people became paralyzed by the fear of failure. . . . His attitude taught me to define failure as not trying something I want to do instead of not achieving the right outcome." Sara practiced what she learned from her dad—failing forward. In fact, Spanx would not exist if she had not failed her LSAT. Sara said, "Everyone has a multimillion-dollar idea inside them. Edison said, 'Genius is one percent inspiration and 99 percent perspiration.'" Sara followed her purpose, maintained a powerful attitude, defined failure on her terms, turned difficulties into opportunities, and took risks by following her passion. She *chose* to get gritty!

GET GRITTY

GET PURPOSE

MASTER THOUGHTS

KNOW SELF

DOMINATE CONTROLLABLES

OWN THE MOMENT

CHOOSE EMOTIONS

OWN WHO YOU ARE

LIVE AND LET GO

COURAGE ZONE

I use Angela Duckworth's definition of grit: "passion and sustained persistence applied toward your long-term goals." I use this definition because it is widely accepted, and the impact of grit has been found to be life changing. Let me explain: When you are gritty, you are tenacious—sticking with your interests over long periods of time. You stay the course despite obstacles, failures, rejections, or negativity. You appreciate the positive factors of a situation even though it may be difficult or stressful. You don't let distractions get in the way of your goals—building the business of your dreams, for example. Your passion comes from an intrinsic interest in your work and craft. You know your work is meaningful and helps others. You perseverance allows you to be resilient in the face of adversity. You have a devotion and unwavering commitment to continuous improvement. When you are gritty, you stick with commitments to your vision, yourself, and others. You don't give up hope. You do what it takes to serve.

The Power of Grit in Your Business

Ever wondered why you might not notice the hours you put in or the sacrifices you make to build your business? The magic ingredient is your grit. As an entrepreneur, salesperson, or leader, you likely wear several hats. You are stretched far beyond your comfort zone and likely feel as if you don't have the time for the high-level goals that keep you awake at night. It's easier to focus on the daily items that are easier to check off your list than it is to focus on the more important long-term items—the game-changing tasks that enable growth in your business and life.

Grit has been described as the number one predictor of long-term success. It is also an essential ingredient in your being open to change and growth. Grit *is* the determining factor between giving up and staying committed and passionate about your business, regardless of obstacles. It is *the* game changer in your life and business, because it is a robust predictor of both work performance and educational performance.

The Power of Grit

Grit has been connected to the following:

- Higher grade point average

- Higher level of education completed

- More earnings

- Openness to learning new systems or persuing new ventures

- Better retention in the workplace

- More engagement at work

- Higher sales performance

- Stronger ability to overcome setbacks

- Better transition to new roles/positions

- More entrepreneurial innovation

- Less addiction

- Longer marriages

- Higher self-efficacy

- More life satisfaction and happiness

- Stronger overall psychological well-being, including more positive affect/emotions

- Less work stress

- Less workplace burnout

- Reduced susceptibility to distractions

- More forgiveness of ourselves and others

GET
GRITTY

GET
PURPOSE

MASTER
THOUGHTS

KNOW
SELF

DOMINATE
CONTROLLABLES

OWN THE
MOMENT

CHOOSE
EMOTIONS

OWN WHO
YOU ARE

LIVE AND
LET GO

COURAGE
ZONE

As you can see from the benefits of grit listed above, grit has been connected to success in both education *and* business as well as psychology. In general, gritty people tend to reach higher ranks of leadership. Sales teams with grit have higher sales performance because they are able to overcome obstacles. For entrepreneurs, grit has been found to be related to innovation and pursuing new ventures. Grit has been shown to predispose people *away* from harmful life choices we can make like internet addiction, gambling, and excessive spending.

Developing your grit is a must!

Grit is the Base of High Performance

How can we explain these strong findings about grit? Along their journeys, the gritty develop other qualities that are essential to high performance. For example, researchers have found that grit is related to several empowering emotions (outlined in chapter 7), such as self-efficacy, life satisfaction, and positive affect and happiness. The more grit you have, the less likely you are to burn out of your job. People that are gritty also report strong self-control, emotional stability, and mental toughness. And, equally as powerful, having grit helps you forgive yourself and others (see chapter 9). When you are gritty, you develop attributes that help you lead a great life and build the business you desire. High performance starts with developing your grit.

Developing Your Grit as a Leader

If grit is so important to our success, how do we develop it, and can it even *be* developed? Yes, it can! Grit is teachable and malleable. While in the trenches helping people develop their grit, I've seen the following:

GET
PURPOSE

MASTER
THOUGHTS

KNOW
SELF

DOMINATE
CONTROLLABLES

OWN THE
MOMENT

CHOOSE
EMOTIONS

OWN WHO
YOU ARE

LIVE AND
LET GO

COURAGE
ZONE

- *Grit starts with understanding what you really, really, really want, both short-term and long-term, for both you and your business.* Why are you the right person to own your business? What's your endgame? What does success mean for you and your business? Do you put the most important things front and center each day?

- *Grit is manifested by working toward long-term goals—those that take years or months to achieve—which is one of the most rewarding things you can do in your business (and your personal life).* What big goals are you working toward? What will take years and years of hard work, dedication, and sacrifice to build?

- *Grit is powered by your purpose and owning it each day.* Why do you do what you do? How do you live your purpose through your business? How do you serve others with what you do or deliver?

- *Grit is fueled by the empowering emotions you need as an entrepreneur and leader: optimism, hope, confidence, and especially gratitude.* How do you prime your emotions each day? Can you manage your focus and see the opportunity in the difficulty? Do you choose to feel good even when things are hard?

- *Grit is ignited by an unwavering commitment to powerful self-talk about yourself and your business's potential.* Have you developed the confidence to choose courage over comfort each day? What's your daily self-talk like about yourself and your business? How do you remind yourself that you have the skills and resources to lead your business?

- *Grit is powered by compassion for and forgiveness of yourself and others.* Can you bounce back and move on quickly when things don't go perfectly in your business? Are you kind and compassionate to yourself when failure happens?

When you cultivate your grit each day, you know exactly where you want to go—and you get there quicker.

Developing Grit in Your Business

Grit can be developed at the organizational level of your business. To build a gritty team, start by selecting and hiring gritty people *and* developing the grit of the people you already have. Gritty organizations have the same traits as gritty people: they are clear about their goals, keep their purpose front and center, choose positive and empowering energy, are compassionate with one another and themselves, have a desire to work hard, and persevere despite adversity and setbacks. Gritty people within an organization also understand specifically who and how they serve their clients or customers, and they relentlessly focus on improving both themselves and their organization. They stay the course to develop the best outcome for their clients or customers. Gritty organizations are focused on service and committed to a shared purpose. A leader developing a gritty team must personify and model passion, compassion, optimism, and perseverance as well as provide relentless communication of the goals, vision, and purpose.

There are many ways to grow your grit, and most of them center around purpose, passion, and the pursuit of goals. As we explore your purpose, passion, and goals below, we'll also assemble the pieces of what I call your Game-Changing Business Road Map, so watch for those prompts.

Your Game-Changing Business Road Map

Your Game-Changing Business Road Map includes six parts:

1. Your Limitless Vision Statement

2. A list of your 10 Stretch Goals

3. Your Game-Changing Goal

4. Five ways to achieve your Game-Changing Goal

5. What you are giving up to reach your Limitless Vision

6. What you need to believe to reach your Limitless Vision

Read on for more details.

Visualize Your Best Possible Self

Grit starts with understanding what you really, really want for your business. This can be one of the most difficult questions for people to answer. But not you. You are a high performer. You are gritty. You do difficult things. We need to get clear on what we want, then figure out how to get there. The desire must come first, and the *how* follows. If you think too quickly about the *how* following the desire, or at the same time, you can get stuck. So, to focus your grit, let's consider your dream and desire.

We are going to do a Best Possible Self (BPS) exercise, which is meant to help you (1) unlock a vision of where you want to go and the road you want to take; (2) think about, and get clear on, who you want to become; and (3) start your Game-Changing Business Road Map. I first encountered the BPS exercise in a meta-analysis study by Johannes Bodo Heekerens and Michael Eid of the Freie Universität Berlin, where they tested the impact of engaging in this written exercise on mood and optimism.

GET GRITTY

GET PURPOSE

MASTER THOUGHTS

KNOW SELF

DOMINATE CONTROLLABLES

OWN THE MOMENT

CHOOSE EMOTIONS

OWN WHO YOU ARE

LIVE AND LET GO

COURAGE ZONE

They included thirty-four studies, with a combined total of 2,627 participants, and found that engaging in the BPS exercise resulted in a measurable increase in optimism and positive affect.

A follow-up study they conducted with 188 psychology undergrads provided similar conclusions—that, compared to the control group, completing the exercise improved positive affect and expectations about the future as well as reduced goal ambivalence, which is the feeling that a goal may not be worth pursuing. In other words, completing the BPS exercise improved several attributes connected to their grit! And the results lasted; they were the same both right after the exercise and a week later.

To complete the BPS exercise, consider the following visualization, which I adapted from the studies mentioned above:

Think about where your life and business will be sometime in the future, perhaps five or ten years from now. Imagine, in detail, everything going the way you would like, the best outcome possible: You worked hard, stayed gritty, and achieved your goals for yourself and your business. Perhaps you started your dream company, realized your financial goals, and/or purchased your dream home, where you now live happily with your family. Imagine it in detail, and sit with it for a while. How do you feel, in body and mind? Who are you with? Where are you at? What have you accomplished?

Now, spend ten minutes writing down everything you imagined. As you are writing, try to be as detailed and specific as possible. Go big! (And remember to turn off your inner critic.)

There is plenty of research that demonstrates the power of this exercise, including one study by Hal Hershfield, a psychologist at UCLA. Hershfield found that when we consider our future self, we make better decisions, including saving more money. As Caroline Adams Miller describes in her book *Getting Grit*, this exercise helps us engage in *mental contrasting*, which is the practice of considering our future self, then coming back to the present, where we can contemplate the obstacles standing in our way and recommit to taking the first step, which may have been seen as overwhelming before.

Your Limitless Vision Statement

After visualizing your future, the next step in developing your grit and your Game-Changing Business Road Map is to write a Limitless Vision Statement that describes exactly where you are going. A Limitless Vision Statement helps you stay gritty and develop life-changing passion. Your vision should get you fired up about your business and trigger an emotional response within you. Your vision allows others to see the possibilities that you see. As a gritty leader, a vision statement helps you communicate the exciting possibilities for the future and the big opportunities you are passionate about. A *Limitless* Vision Statement is your opportunity to describe your big dream while stepping into your potential—which is endless and unlimited. If you put limits on your potential, others will too. If you aren't excited, how will others be? If you aren't passionate, how can you expect people to follow and stay gritty with you?

"If your dreams don't scare you, they aren't big enough."
—Ellen Johnson Sirleaf

GET GRITTY

GET PURPOSE

MASTER THOUGHTS

KNOW SELF

DOMINATE CONTROLLABLES

OWN THE MOMENT

CHOOSE EMOTIONS

OWN WHO YOU ARE

LIVE AND LET GO

COURAGE ZONE

You can hardly exaggerate your vision. Write it wildly, with no limits. Be outrageous! Dream big! A small dream will limit you. A big dream is a prerequisite for reaching your potential, necessary to develop the business of your dreams. Dreaming big means considering all possibilities, turning off comfort and limiting self-talk, and choosing to step into what is calling you. As Steven Spielberg—the award-winning movie director and producer with a net worth of \$3.6 million who is responsible for classic hits such as *Jaws*, *E.T. the Extra-Terrestrial*, and *Gremlins*—once said, "I'm dreaming for a living." He further explained, "My imagination won't turn off. I wake up so excited I can't eat breakfast. I never run out of energy." Dreaming for a living is a necessity for you to reach your destiny. You must dream big *now*, as you write your vision statement, and dream *daily* to keep your passion alive. We all must dream for a living. Your business and future self depend on it.

Start dreaming for a living, and write your Limitless Vision Statement with clarity. First, open your computer or get out a notebook. Answer these five questions about your business and your big dreams:

1. Why are you passionate about your business?

2. Who do you serve in your business?

3. How do you serve those people?

4. What big, outrageous dream or game-changing goal of yours completely lights your fire (think five, ten, fifteen, or twenty years from now)?

5. What will make your business successful over time?

Your Limitless Vision Statement

On _____

(a date five to twenty years from now)

I/we will grow _____

(your business name)

into _____

(big, outrageous goal)

with an annual revenue of $ _____

so that _____

(who you serve)

can _____

(why you serve them)

Now, create a Limitless Vision Statement based on how you answered the above questions.

GET GRITTY

GET PURPOSE

MASTER THOUGHTS

KNOW SELF

DOMINATE CONTROLLABLES

OWN THE MOMENT

CHOOSE EMOTIONS

OWN WHO YOU ARE

LIVE AND LET GO

COURAGE ZONE

YOUR GAME-CHANGING BUSINESS ROADMAP

Your Limitless Vision Statement

Your Game-Changing Goal

To reach my Limitless Vision, I believe . . .

Your Ten Stretch Goals

*Five Ways to Achieve
Your Game-Changing Goal*

*To reach my Limitless Vision,
I give up . . .*

GET
PURPOSE

MASTER
THOUGHTS

KNOW
SELF

DOMINATE
CONTROLLABLES

OWN THE
MOMENT

CHOOSE
EMOTIONS

OWN WHO
YOU ARE

LIVE AND
LET GO

COURAGE
ZONE

Here is an example of my company's Limitless Vision Statement to give you an example:

> On 1/1/2030, we will grow Mentally Strong Consulting into one of the the largest mental-performance companies in the United States, with an annual revenue of at least $3 million, so that business owners, leaders, coaches, and athletes can live their big dreams, reach their potential, and be their best selves more consistently.

And here is another example, from a firm I provide coaching and training to:

> On 1/1/2026, we will have grown our financial firm into the largest company in our region, with an annual revenue of $5 million, so that business owners and families can have the financial planning they deserve and need.

Your Limitless Vision Statement is the first piece of your Game-Changing Business Road Map, so keep it handy as you read on.

Your 10 Stretch Goals

Now that you have written a Limitless Vision Statement and started dreaming intentionally about your business, let's take the next step by documenting your goals as part of your Game-Changing Business Road Map. One of the most robust and replicable findings within the literature on performance psychology is that goals direct your focus, fuel your desire, and help you remain persistent in the face of adversity. A goal is a measurable and desired result you are seeking. The World's Best

GET
PURPOSE

MASTER
THOUGHTS

KNOW
SELF

DOMINATE
CONTROLLABLES

OWN THE
MOMENT

CHOOSE
EMOTIONS

OWN WHO
YOU ARE

LIVE AND
LET GO

COURAGE
ZONE

are goal oriented. They know what they want to accomplish each year, week, day, and meeting. Their long-term goals are connected with their monthly, weekly, and daily goals. These goals fuel them with life-changing passion.

As a leader in your business, if you aren't sure what outcomes you want a year from now or why your clients or customers keep coming back, how will you lead your team with clarity? How will you make sure you keep the most important goals as your daily focus and say no to the less important goals? Which Power Phrases (discussed in chapter 3) will help you consistently focus on how your daily goals connect to your weekly goals, monthly goals, or yearly goals?

Setting goals should get you fired up and inspired. And writing your goals down allows you to document your desires and think like the World's Best. The only way to completely own where you want to go is to write it. If you don't write your goals down, your goals will likely be forgotten and ignored. The World's Best have their goals inked!

Your goals should also be difficult to accomplish. On episode 418 of the *High Performance Mindset* podcast, I spoke with Caroline Adams Miller, author of *Getting Grit*. We had a great conversation about hard goals. I loved what she said: "The happiest people wake up every day to really hard goals, not easy goals. The good kind of grit is going after hard goals, going out of your comfort zone, taking risks and doing it for an extended amount of time." What hard goals are *you* going after?

Now that your mind is thinking big, let's stretch it out and create the next piece of your Game-Changing Business Road Map. Open up your computer or grab a notebook, then answer the question below, giving yourself eight to ten minutes, considering the hard goals you want to go after (and read on to help you think about your goals):

What are ten stretch goals for my business five or ten years from now?

What goals would stretch you and help you step into your potential? A stretch goal helps you move beyond your current capabilities and performance. It requires sacrifice, dreaming big, and grit, and it should push you toward new possibilities, feeding the fire in your belly. A stretch goal may even be a little uncomfortable to pursue. It might include a new approach or a brand-new path. What hard, gritty goals do you want to pursue?

Now, I know what happens when people answer the stretch-goal question. I've seen it in my Beyond Grit Live events and within my group coaching and mastermind groups. Even though it says "stretch goals," people still have a tendency to dream small. But not you! Fight your natural inclination to dream small. Choose courage instead. Remember: we all need hard goals to go after. Dream as you would encourage a friend to dream. Dream as you would encourage your child to dream. Dream knowing you deserve to dream. Dream as if your business will change at least one million lives. As you are writing this list, think *what*, not *how*. If your mind starts thinking, *How will I do that?* redirect it back to *what* you want to do. Stay focused on the *what*. Have fun exploring all the possibilities!

Add your 10 Stretch Goals to your Game-Changing Business Road Map.

GET
GRITTY

GET
PURPOSE

MASTER
THOUGHTS

KNOW
SELF

DOMINATE
CONTROLLABLES

OWN THE
MOMENT

CHOOSE
EMOTIONS

OWN WHO
YOU ARE

LIVE AND
LET GO

COURAGE
ZONE

Share your story and/or any part of your Game-Changing Business Road Map with us via email at cindra@cindrakamphoff.com, or tag me in your Instagram Stories using @CindraKamphoff. Sharing with others helps you believe it will become reality! I can't wait to read your Limitless Vision Statement and goals.

Your Game-Changing Goal

Now that you have your list of stretch goals written, let's consider your outcome and your process. Your *outcome* is the final product you seek, and your *process* is how you get there. To consider your outcome, ask yourself, *Which single goal that I have written down would get me to my dream the fastest, move the needle for my business, or have the biggest overall impact?* I call this your Game-Changing Goal. For example, your Game-Changing Goal could be to write a book, develop a new life-changing product, launch a new profit center in your business, hire X amount of new employees, or add X number of new clients. Circle that goal on your list and write "Game Changer" by it. And if your Game-Changing Goal is not written in a specific and measurable way, rewrite it with more specific language. Again, this is the question you should ask:

What is my Game-Changing Goal, the one that would help me get to my five- or ten-year dream the quickest?

After you have circled your Game-Changing Goal (and added it to your Game-Changing Business Road Map), making sure it is specific and measurable, consider the *how*. Yes, finally, this is the time to consider your *how*! The *how* is your process.

The process is important to consider the actions that you need to take on a daily or weekly basis to reach your Game-Changing Goal. Focusing on the process and writing several process goals improves your confidence, reduces your anxiety, and gives you a clear plan of action. If your Game-Changing Goal is to write a book, your process may include deciding on the topic, outlining the chapters, writing each day for at least thirty minutes, finding a publisher, and developing a marketing plan. Write down your thoughts to this big question:

What are five ways to achieve my Game-Changing Goal?

Write down at least five ideas, even if you aren't sure you want to move forward with them, even if you think an idea is impossible. Be an idea-generating machine, considering the ways you could achieve that Game-Changing Goal. Once you have that list, ask yourself this question:

What's my starting point to get me closer to my Game-Changing Goal? (Circle it.)

Once you've settled on five solid ways to achieve your Game-Changing Goal, add them to your Game-Changing Business Road Map before moving on.

Great! Now let's consider the blocks that might hold you back.

Beliefs to Support Your Game-Changing Goal

You will encounter plenty of obstacles and setbacks on your way toward reaching your vision and accomplishing your goals, including your Game-Changing Goal. Some of those obstacles and setbacks will be outside events or the actions of others that you cannot control. Based on my experience coaching business leaders, however, the majority of obstacles will most likely be controllable factors or internal blocks and barriers related to your mindset. Here's a question to consider to help you reflect on the internal blocks that could get in your way:

What do I need to give up to reach my Limitless Vision for my business?

For example, you might need to reduce internal barriers (judgment of yourself or others, self-doubt, procrastination, etc.) and/or time barriers (social media use, lunches with friends, etc.). Add your answer to your Game-Changing Business Road Map. Lastly, let's consider your mindset and the internal beliefs you need to adopt to reach your Limitless Vision and your Game-Changing Goal.

What do you need to believe to reach your Limitless Vision?

Consider the most important thought or belief you need to adopt or remind yourself of to reach your Limitless Vision. Perhaps it is a thought or belief about yourself as a leader, or about your ability to build a business that reaches your vision. It could also be a belief about the world or the people that work for you. Think big and powerful as you write this thought or belief. Examples include the following:

GET GRITTY

GET PURPOSE

MASTER THOUGHTS

KNOW SELF

DOMINATE CONTROLLABLES

OWN THE MOMENT

CHOOSE EMOTIONS

OWN WHO YOU ARE

LIVE AND LET GO

COURAGE ZONE

- "I am a confident and powerful leader."

- "I can do hard and difficult things."

- "I am meant to lead this company."

- "My people need my leadership."

- "Opportunity is coming my way."

Here are four key mindset shifts you can use if you feel stuck:

- **Mindset Shift 1:** Setbacks and adversity are a given; it is how you respond to these obstacles that makes all the difference. Next time you experience a setback or adversity, consider how the difficulty is happening *for* you, not *to* you. When you consider how it is happening *for* you, it can be viewed as a gift that will help you grow or learn. You take a creator approach to the difficulty, instead of a victim approach. Your business is impacted by the meaning you give events. Focus on the gains, and find empowering meaning in each difficult moment or failure.

- **Mindset Shift 2:** Thinking that building your dream business to meet your vision will come easily will leave you ill prepared. If you underestimate how difficult it will be to achieve something, you'll feel intimidated later on and maybe even give up. It's easier to tap into your grit if you anticipate difficulty in advance. What difficulties might you experience as you work toward your Limitless Vision? How do you plan to approach those difficulties? What is your planned reaction or strategy? Have grit—don't quit!

- **Mindset Shift 3:** Continue developing your Game-Changing Business Road Map. What can you regularly do to reach your Limitless Vision? What big three goals will you pursue this year? According to the research on goal setting, approximately three goals is an ideal amount for you to focus on at any given time. Which less important goals do you need to give up? How will you align your monthly goals with your weekly and daily goals? The clearer your Game-Changing Business Road Map is, the easier it will be to implement. Write out as many details as possible.

- **Mindset Shift 4:** Know that you will get off track. According to my good friend Shannon Huffman Polson—one of the first women to fly the Apache helicopter in the US Army and author of *The Grit Factor*—if a pilot is a little off course, over time they will end up a very long way from their destination. Building a business and reaching your vision is not a straight line, and if you are a little off course at the beginning, you will end up at a completely different destination than you intended. What will you do to get clear on where you want to go? And how will you know if you get off course? When faced with an obstacle, what will be your plan to deal with it?

Remember, when you cultivate your grit, you'll get to your Limitless Vision quicker. You'll have more energy to sustain you and your business over years and decades. Success is about sustained performance over time, and cultivating your grit each day is necessary to do so.

GET GRITTY

GET PURPOSE

MASTER THOUGHTS

KNOW SELF

DOMINATE CONTROLLABLES

OWN THE MOMENT

CHOOSE EMOTIONS

OWN WHO YOU ARE

LIVE AND LET GO

COURAGE ZONE

You should now have all six components of your Game-Changing Business Road Map:

1. Your Limitless Vision Statement

2. A list of your 10 Stretch Goals

3. Your Game-Changing Goal

4. Five ways to achieve your Game-Changing Goal

5. What you are giving up on to reach your Limitless Vision

6. What you need to believe to reach your Limitless Vision

You'll want to keep these components on one sheet of paper, to guide you so that you make daily decisions that align with your Road Map. To keep these components together, you can download the Game-Changing Business Road Map guide at beyondgrit.com or add them to your Grit Board (see box).

**Exercise: Make a Grit Board
to Guide Your Business**

*To help you reach your
Limitless Vision and develop
the persistence to get to
where you want to go,
develop a Grit Board.*

All you need to get started is an 11 x 17 inch poster
board. Keep it handy as you proceed with this book.

You can start by including all of the components of
your Game-Changing Business Road Map on your Grit
Board. At the end of each chapter, you'll find insights
to record on your Grit Board.

When you are finished with your Grit Board, at the
end of the book, put it in your office or workspace to
guide you daily.

You can find instructions and examples of Grit Boards
at beyondgrit.com.

GET
PURPOSE

MASTER
THOUGHTS

KNOW
SELF

DOMINATE
CONTROLLABLES

OWN THE
MOMENT

CHOOSE
EMOTIONS

OWN WHO
YOU ARE

LIVE AND
LET GO

COURAGE
ZONE

My High Performance Game Plan
GET GRITTY

1. I will dream for a living and write my Limitless Vision Statement in order to drive me to build the business that will provide me with all that I desire emotionally, financially, and mentally.

2. I will create a Game-Changing Business Road Map and include a list of my 10 Stretch Goals for my business for the next five or ten years.

3. I will determine my ultimate Game-Changing Goal, the one goal that will have the biggest impact and get me to my Limitless Vision the fastest.

4. Finally, after being an idea-generating machine, I will determine my starting point to get closer to my ultimate Game-Changing Goal.

Now, take a moment to record the following on your Grit Board:

- Your Limitless Vision Statement

- 10 Stretch Goals five or ten years from now

- Your ultimate Game-Changing Goal

My High Performance Power Phrase:

**I am gritty. I am passionate and have
a clear vision of the life I am building.**

2

Get Clear on Your Purpose

The World's Best own why they do what they do. They keep their why front and center. This purpose keeps them motivated and hungry when the going gets tough.

Chapter 2

Get Clear
on Your Purpose

"Service is the rent we pay for being. It is the very purpose of life, and not something you do in your spare time."
—MARIAN WRIGHT EDELMAN, ENTREPRENEUR

Angie Bastian and her husband, Dan, started popping kettle corn in their garage in 2001 to start a college fund for their two children. When I had her on the *High Performance Mindset Podcast*, she said, "We come from the belief that education is the avenue and foundation for success and for creating a situation that gives a child the benefit of everything that is possible." They started selling their kettle corn in front of grocery stores, at high school events, and at other amateur sporting events—anywhere they could. Dan is a huge Minnesota Vikings fan, so when the Vikings came to town for training camp, Angie asked him, "Don't you think it'd be fun, like, if the Vikings ate our popcorn?" They contacted the Vikings the next day, and the team was happy to accept free kettle corn. Angie and Dan dropped off 120 bags for the players to eat while they watched film. There was such a buzz among the players and staff the next day that the Vikings asked Angie and Dan if they wanted their product to become the official kettle corn of the Minnesota Vikings. Angie said, "What we didn't know at the time was that we were marketing to influencers. You know, we had no idea, but it was an instinct, and we followed it." Angie's BOOMCHICKAPOP is now one of the fastest-growing popcorn brands in the world.

When I asked Angie how she stayed mentally fueled to grow the business, she described how Viktor Frankl's book *Man's Search for Meaning* helped her to understand purpose. In the highly influential book, Frankl, a neurologist and psychiatrist, described his experiences as an inmate in a concentration camp during the Holocaust. He argued that we can find meaning in all forms, even in the most brutal conditions, and that the meaning of life is found in every moment, even in suffering and death. "Life is never made unbearable by circumstances," he wrote, "but only by lack of meaning and purpose." Angie, who you heard from in the preface of this book, said she was clear on her purpose: "It's all about the team, the people you bring into your system, the integrity and quality of your product. But most important, it's about the people, the connections, and the relationships." Without the focus on their team, Angie and Dan would likely not have built their popcorn company into what it is today (they recently sold it for $250 million).

Owning Your Purpose in Your Business

Understanding your *why* and purpose is critical to building the business of your dreams as an entrepreneur, salesperson, and/or business leader. Imagine two business owners: one owner builds their business just to pay the bills, whereas the other owner wakes up "on fire" each morning, with a sense of service and purpose as well as a focus on using their gifts to positively impact the world. Over time, the difference between these two owners and their businesses is night and day, as the second owner owns not only their business—but their purpose.

Energy is a *must* if you want to realize your vision and accomplish your goals, and acting with energy starts with owning your *why* and purpose. One study of elite athletes shows us the power of

GET GRITTY

GET PURPOSE

MASTER THOUGHTS

KNOW SELF

DOMINATE CONTROLLABLES

OWN THE MOMENT

CHOOSE EMOTIONS

OWN WHO YOU ARE

LIVE AND LET GO

COURAGE ZONE

purpose and how purpose relates to energy and performance: Dr. Ben Houltberg and his colleagues found that elite athletes who had a purpose-based identity (focused on living their purpose, with a positive view of the future) had higher levels of life satisfaction and fewer psychological disruptions—depression, anxiety, shame, etc.—compared to those who had a performance-based identity (focused on winning, with greater concern over mistakes and higher fear of failure).

Getting clarity on your purpose is key for you to not only realize your vision but also feel empowered along the way. If you don't understand and live your purpose, you can get off track, burn out, and feel unfulfilled building your business. Your purpose allows you to be absorbed in the moment, have the freedom to take risks, and be your authentic self more often.

Your purpose is your cause, or the reason(s) you do what you do. Your purpose is the reason you wake up in the morning. Your purpose is the reason your business exists. Your purpose is what makes you human, and it cannot be taken from you. Owning and understanding your purpose can also help you figure out *how* to achieve your vision for your business. As German philosopher Friedrich Nietzsche once said, "He who has a *why* can endure any *how*." When you are feeling overwhelmed or frustrated, your purpose can help you focus on what matters most, compel you to take risks, and fuel you in lonely times while building your business—staying gritty regardless of odds or obstacles. Your courage is fueled by your purpose. You need courage each and every day to build your business toward your big, audacious, limitless vision. Owning your purpose is necessary as a business leader.

Owning your purpose means three things:

1. **Reminding yourself—every day—why you do what you do, to stay intrinsically motivated, courageous, and gritty.** Some leaders consider it their core purpose to have a positive influence on the lives of others, whereas other leaders consider it their core purpose to demonstrate that anything is possible, living life fully as an example.

2. **Communicating your purpose to your ideal clients, your colleagues, and others around you so they connect with you.** You might communicate your purpose through a robust onboarding protocol for new clients, have a clear operating process that reflects your values and vision, or unapologetically weave your purpose into your branding, sales funnels, and training materials for new hires.

3. **Using your purpose to inform your decisions, including what you say yes to and no to.** In order to stay focused and reach your vision, you will need to say no to less important goals and reduce or eliminate distractions. As Stephen R. Covey suggested in his book *The 7 Habits of Highly Effective People*, you will need to put first things first to reach your big vision.

I've found that the most successful business leaders, entrepreneurs, and salespeople own their *why* in all three of these ways. They wake up on fire with their purpose in focus, share their purpose regularly, and use it to guide their daily actions.

Finding Your Reason for Being

Several years ago, I came across a concept called *ikigai* (pronounced "ee-kee-guy"), a Japanese term that loosely

GET GRITTY

GET PURPOSE

MASTER THOUGHTS

KNOW SELF

DOMINATE CONTROLLABLES

OWN THE MOMENT

CHOOSE EMOTIONS

OWN WHO YOU ARE

LIVE AND LET GO

COURAGE ZONE

translates to "reason for being." According to those born on Okinawa (an island between Taiwan and Japan), ikigai refers to the reason we get up in the morning. Some people have found their ikigai, while others are still searching for theirs, even though we each carry it with us. It takes reflection and awareness to understand and live according to your ikigai. Since I first encountered this concept several years ago, I've worked to apply it to myself and my business, and I've shared it with many of my clients. When you have a clearly defined ikigai, you feel happier and more satisfied, and have more meaning in your life.

Through the lens of ikigai, a meaningful life and business is found in the balance between four areas: (1) what you love, (2) what you are good at, (3) what the world needs, and (4) what you can be paid for.

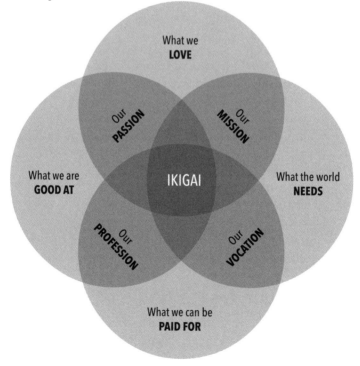

To live your best life and continue to build a business that fuels you, you need to first find what you're most passionate about, what you are willing to fight for, what you can do that others cannot, and what you are uniquely positioned to offer—then consider the ways you can express that passion.

Think of a time in the past when you were so engrossed in what you were doing that you lost track of time. This gives you a clue about what your calling may be and what you are uniquely positioned to offer. Psychologist Mihaly Csikszentmihalyi, author of the bestselling book *Flow: The Psychology of Optimal Experience*, has termed the concept "flow." Flow happens when you are completely absorbed in an activity, working within your "zone of genius," where you are most connected to your unique gifts.

To apply ikigai and understand what you are uniquely positioned to offer the world, consider your answers to these questions:

- What do you love?
- What are you good at?
- What does the world need?
- What can you be paid for?

When I applied it to myself, I discovered these answers:

- **What do you love?** – Mindset training, reading, learning, big ideas, and guiding others.

- **What are you good at?** – Providing tangible strategies and tools, backed by research, that make a difference in people's lives.

- **What does the world need?** – Mindset training on how to move forward with more courage and less fear, helping people and their businesses succeed.

- **What can you be paid for?** – Speaking, writing, coaching, workshops, and mastermind groups.

GET GRITTY

GET PURPOSE

MASTER THOUGHTS

KNOW SELF

DOMINATE CONTROLLABLES

OWN THE MOMENT

CHOOSE EMOTIONS

OWN WHO YOU ARE

LIVE AND LET GO

COURAGE ZONE

Write out the four questions on paper or using a computer, and answer them. Or you can draw your own ikigai diagram and fill it in with your answers. There is also a blank ikigai diagram below, to use as you like.

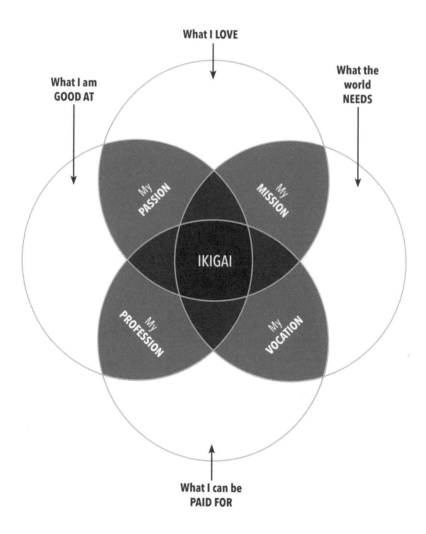

All four questions are important to answer, but *What does the world need?* is a powerful one because it highlights the importance of understanding the value your business provides in the lives of others.

Servant leadership, a term coined by Robert K. Greenleaf, is a "philosophy and set of practices that enriches the lives of individuals, builds better organizations and ultimately creates a more just and caring world." Servant leadership begins with seeking to serve and to better others' lives. We each need to keep service front and center as we work to reach our vision. If we don't, we act in selfish ways or get in our own way, adopting a victim mindset.

Service, or giving to others, is also a powerful component of purpose. As said by Richard Leider, author of *The Power of Purpose*, we become the best version of ourselves when our purpose is larger than ourselves. On episode 333 of the *High Performance Mindset* podcast, Richard also shared that we live seven to ten years longer when we live our purpose. Our purpose is vital for our health, happiness, and well-being.

We all have the need to matter. How does what you do help, inspire, and provide for others? We achieve our deepest satisfaction when we desire to make a difference in the world. When we understand and express our gifts in the interest and for the sake of others, we feel fully alive. If you go through life without offering your gifts to others, you can experience frustration, burnout, and even depression. How do you (or will you) serve, provide value, and give of your talents to others? A key component to building the business of your dreams is to add more value than anyone else. Keeping those you serve front and center will help drive your intrinsic motivation, maintain your fire, and ultimately create the biggest impact for your ideal client.

GET GRITTY

GET PURPOSE

MASTER THOUGHTS

KNOW SELF

DOMINATE CONTROLLABLES

OWN THE MOMENT

CHOOSE EMOTIONS

OWN WHO YOU ARE

LIVE AND LET GO

COURAGE ZONE

Understanding Your Ideal Client

As a business leader, entrepreneur, and/or salesperson, it is essential to understand, in detail, who your ideal client is, how to sell your product or service to them, and how to satisfy them so they keep buying from you again and again. I've seen evidence of this in my coaching practice: when entrepreneurs aren't sure who their ideal client is and try to attract everyone, they attract no one.

For example, when I first started to coach Brittany, she was recording podcast episodes, developing products, and marketing her business on social media, all without a clear understanding of her ideal client. Few people would listen, engage, or buy. When she got clear that her ideal clients were new moms ages twenty-five to thirty-five, her business started to skyrocket.

Your ideal client is a person who gets one or more exact needs met by the product or service you offer. The more clarity you have about who your ideal client is, the more focused and effective you will be in serving the world. Understanding your ideal client is essential for the future of your business and for your ability to operate according to your ikigai. I've found that business owners and leaders can be anxious about getting crystal clear about their ideal client, for fear of excluding others. The key is to remember that with more clarity comes more business.

Consider a time you went fishing or when one of your friends, clients, or family members told you a story about going fishing. If you know the exact fish you want to catch, what time they typically bite, and where they typically bite, you are more likely to catch the type of fish you desire. The same is true for attracting your ideal client. The more you know about your ideal client—their desires, struggles, and perspectives—the easier it will be to reach them. To better understand your ideal client, consider the CAMP Formula:

C:

Characteristics: What are the characteristics of your ideal client? How old are they? Where do they live geographically? Where do they work? What are their interests and hobbies? What is their level of education and average income?

A:

Ambition: What are your ideal client's ambitions or desires? What do they want out of life? What are the obstacles or barriers to achieving what they desire? What do they need from you and your business that they couldn't produce or do alone? How can you help them overcome the obstacles in their path?

M:

My Purpose: How do your ideal client's desires match with your purpose, or ikigai? Why should your ideal client buy from you over others?

P:

Pain Points: What are your ideal client's biggest pain points? What do they fear? What do they struggle with the most? What specific pain point or problem does your business address?

GET
GRITTY

GET
PURPOSE

MASTER
THOUGHTS

KNOW
SELF

DOMINATE
CONTROLLABLES

OWN THE
MOMENT

CHOOSE
EMOTIONS

OWN WHO
YOU ARE

LIVE AND
LET GO

COURAGE
ZONE

Writing Your Business Purpose Statement

Let's take this one step further by writing a purpose statement to help you live according to your ikigai and build the business you envision. To write a purpose statement that will guide your work and business, consider your answers to these four *W*'s (keeping in mind your answers to the CAMP question above):

- *Who* is your ideal client?

- *What* products or services do you provide to your ideal client?

- *What* value do you provide for your ideal client?

- *Why* do you serve your ideal client?

Insert your answers into the blanks in the sentence below, and feel free to modify the structure if it feels too constrained:

The purpose of _____
(name of your business)

is to provide _____
(products or services you offer)

to _____
(describe your ideal client)

so that _____
(value you provide)

and _____
(why you serve your ideal client)

As with writing a *personal* purpose statement (which I covered in *Beyond Grit*), the purpose statement for your business should do the following:

- Energize you every time you read it, say it, or share it.

- Be a purpose you can experience daily.

- Include gritty words that are powerful and big.

- Focus on what you *do* want, not on what you *don't* want.

- Impact others beyond yourself.

- Be simple enough to memorize.

- Be specific and avoid words that are universal, such as *always* and *never*.

Look at the purpose statement you created, and ask yourself, *Deep down, does this inspire me to do what I do? Would this get me fired up each morning? Does it include big, powerful, gritty words that describe my passion?* If your answered *Yes* to all three questions, yippee! You have an incredible first draft of your purpose statement. If you answered *No* to any of them, play with the words or structure until you can answer in the affirmative. Replace words that don't fuel your fire with ones that do. It may take some time.

Here are a few examples of my clients' businesses' purpose statements to inspire you:

- The purpose of our practice is to provide education and foresight through lifelong holistic financial-planning relationships to individuals and closely held business owners within ten years of retirement so that they can find true peace and create multigenerational wealth that enriches our communities (financial services company).

GET GRITTY

GET PURPOSE

MASTER THOUGHTS

KNOW SELF

DOMINATE CONTROLLABLES

OWN THE MOMENT

CHOOSE EMOTIONS

OWN WHO YOU ARE

LIVE AND LET GO

COURAGE ZONE

- The purpose of our business is to provide coaching and consulting to new business owners, new leaders, and their teams so they can break through their biggest limitations and get a clear direction for their future success in life and in their business (coaching and consulting company).

- The purpose of our business is to build lasting relationships, offer cutting-edge advice, and provide education to families and business owners so they can have peace of mind and financial protection, allowing them to work on what matters most in their lives (financial services company).

- The purpose of our business is to provide solutions and safely deliver quality and innovative metal products to equipment manufacturers nationwide so that they can power the world, build America's highways, propel the US Navy, and so much more (manufacturing company).

And here is my business's purpose statement:

- The purpose of Mentally Strong Consulting is to provide workshops, coaching, and keynotes to business leaders, executives, and high-level athletes so they can live and work with clarity and mental strength and discover their unlimited potential.

Own Your Story

Now that you have written the purpose statement for your business, let's consider why you are uniquely positioned to serve your ideal client. What have you experienced in the past that led you to this purpose?

Owning your story will help you connect with your business and purpose in a deeper way. It allows you to feel proud of the difficulties, obstacles, and struggles you have overcome, because those exact experiences have led you to serve the way you do. Owning your story will allow you to turn your mess into your mess*age*, your trials into your tri*umphs*, your breakdowns into your break*throughs*. Owning, or being proud of, your story demonstrates vulnerability, trust, and confidence, which can motivate others to connect with you and your business, maybe sharing their stories as well.

When you own your story, you also take control of the meaning you attach to your struggles and difficulties, which you can then use to serve. Owning your story means that you don't feel ashamed, powerless, or guilty about your difficulties and struggles, that you've released any guilt or negativity—that your difficulties and struggles happened *for* you, not *to* you. You are empowered to use your struggle for good. As Brené Brown said in her book *Daring Greatly*, "When we deny the story, it defines us. When we own the story, we can write a brave new ending."

Here are four questions to help you consider how sharing your story will help you reach your ideal client:

1. What successes led you to this business?

2. What struggles led you to this business?

3. What did you learn from your successes and struggles that you want to share with others?

4. How can you use your story to best serve your clients?

Your purpose fuels your grit and makes you unique. Remember, no one else has the same mix of experiences, talents, gifts, desires, and dreams as you. No one can offer the world what you can, fueled with your struggles and powered by your story. Identifying your purpose today and then honoring it is perhaps the most important step that you will take toward high performance!

GET GRITTY

GET PURPOSE

MASTER THOUGHTS

KNOW SELF

DOMINATE CONTROLLABLES

OWN THE MOMENT

CHOOSE EMOTIONS

OWN WHO YOU ARE

LIVE AND LET GO

COURAGE ZONE

My High Performance Game Plan
GET CLEAR
ON YOUR PURPOSE

1. I will own my purpose by reminding myself, each day, why I do what I do.

2. I will determine my ikigai, my reason for being, which includes what I love, what I am good at, what the world needs, and what I can be paid for.

3. I will identify my ideal client in detail, knowing it will be easier to continue to reach and serve them.

4. Finally, I will own my story by turning my mess into my mess*age*, my trials into my tri*umphs*, and my breakdowns into my break*throughs*.

Now, take a moment to record the following on your Grit Board:

- Your purpose statement
- A completed diagram of your ikigai

My High Performance Power Phrase:

I know my reason for being.
I own my purpose and live it each day.

3

Master Your Thoughts

The World's Best

are intentional with their self-talk.
They exhibit powerful, positive, and
possibility-oriented thoughts
focused on the process.

Chapter 3

Master Your
Thoughts

"Work harder on yourself than you do your job."
—JIM ROHN, AMERICAN BUSINESSMAN AND SELF-MADE MILLIONAIRE

I first met BJ Hellyer, managing partner at a Fortune 100 financial firm, six or seven years ago. I was the keynote speaker at one of his team's quarterly meetings, where I spoke about developing the High Performance Mindset. I was struck by his knowledge of high performance, grit, and self-development. He had read the same books I had, studying the material closely and then teaching it to the advisors at his firm. He could definitely speak the language of high performance.

BJ started as an intern at the firm after graduating from college, and twenty years later, he became a managing partner. I had BJ on the *High Performance Mindset* podcast to learn more about his mindset practices (episode 316). He believes that "leaders are readers," which is why he reads every day. "If I can add value in drips in my conversations with others," he said, "then that gives me credibility as a leader." A key component to his success and ability to lead from his values and principles is his morning routine. He said, "When I set up my environment to master myself and master the morning, then priorities tend to fall into place because I have led the hardest person first—myself."

Lead the hardest person first—you. It can be difficult to lead yourself, for sure. You are working against your brain's hardwiring to show command over yourself—your emotions and attention.

Our brains are hardwired to see what's missing, the negative perspective in any given situation. When we lead ourselves first, we activate our self-command "muscle" and lead in an intentional way. At times, it can feel easier to lead others—to help them hit their deadlines, be on time, and follow through on their commitments. In comparison, it can often feel harder to lead yourself—to ensure you are engaging in a morning routine that primes you, practicing good self-care, and managing any self-trash-talk your brain throws out. The first step of leading yourself, and the heart of your ability to do so, is being aware of your thoughts. What you think about yourself as a leader, you become.

As an executive and performance coach who works one-on-one with people like you, I hear all of the ways we get in our own way. It is common for a client of mine to tell me their deepest thoughts and beliefs that create barriers to their best self, to realizing their vision for their business. We can create these barriers without us realizing it. Awareness is always the first step to mastering your mind, and daily mental conditioning is the next step. Here are a few examples of thoughts that hold my clients back, which we work to debunk and overcome:

- "I'm from a small town, and there is no way I can make the connections required to build this job in sales."

- "No matter what I do, I'll never get a promotion to be VP."

- "The client will probably not give me a referral anyway, so why ask?"

GET GRITTY

GET PURPOSE

MASTER THOUGHTS

KNOW SELF

DOMINATE CONTROLLABLES

OWN THE MOMENT

CHOOSE EMOTIONS

OWN WHO YOU ARE

LIVE AND LET GO

COURAGE ZONE

- "There are so many candidates more qualified than me. There is no reason to speak up."

- "What will they think if I fail at this?"

Could you hear your own inner critic as you read those words? Even if you couldn't, you still experience some version of an inner critic. We all do. Knowing you have an inner critic helps you realize you are not alone, allows you to become more aware of your inner critic's tendencies, and shows you the need to master your inner game and ensure your thoughts work *for* you, not *against* you.

Tony Robbins, a personal-development guru known for his live events and business mastery, famously says that business is 80 percent psychology and 20 percent strategy or skill. That means that 80 percent of your success and ability to reach your vision has to do with the thoughts and focus you allow. Your mind is the engine that drives your mastery— both of yourself and the future you dream of. It powers everything you do, including your emotions, actions, destiny, and legacy. And if you want to power your life and business, achieving your vision, you must guard your mind accordingly.

When you level up your thoughts, you level up your business. Your ability to master your thoughts determines your potential, including both your level of happiness and the income you will make in your business. Mastering yourself involves daily conditioning targeted at helping you notice the thoughts and beliefs holding you back. Once you're in the practice of noticing those limiting thoughts and beliefs daily, then you can start choosing daily focuses—engaging in powerful self-talk and building unstoppable beliefs.

You may think that mastering your mind is like learning to ride a bicycle—that once you learn the strategies discussed in this chapter and book, you won't need to think about them again. But that's dead wrong. Mastering your mind and yourself is *nothing* like riding a bicycle. Instead, each day, you must make time to set your intention to master your mind and lead yourself. You must notice the thoughts and beliefs holding you back and choose powerful self-talk to build beliefs that will help you realize your vision. This daily practice begins with the GRIT Morning Exercise (outlined earlier in this book), followed by some of the other strategies in this book, which together help to keep your mind focused on your purpose, primed with gratitude and energy, and able to move forward with your bold vision.

Powerful Thoughts = Powerful Business

There's no denying the link between thoughts and business performance. If your inner dialogue, or self-talk, is disempowering—sapping vitality from you or your vision for your business—your business will suffer. If your inner dialogue is compassionate, positive, and uplifting, your business will be more likely to flourish.

Your inner dialogue is where your mind interprets your feelings and perceptions of events that impact your life and business as well as where you give yourself reinforcement and instruction. In fact, in a study that appeared in the journal *Human Relations*, Charles Manz and his colleagues shared that lower-performing business leaders reported their thoughts as being focused more on personal deficiencies, whereas higher-performing leaders reported their thoughts as being focused on external factors they could overcome to facilitate personal growth. In an additional study published in the *Journal of Managerial Psychology*, the authors analyzed written letters that executives wrote to themselves. The

GET GRITTY

GET PURPOSE

MASTER THOUGHTS

KNOW SELF

DOMINATE CONTROLLABLES

OWN THE MOMENT

CHOOSE EMOTIONS

OWN WHO YOU ARE

LIVE AND LET GO

COURAGE ZONE

study found that positive, constructive self-talk—e.g., "I am great at my job and should give myself more credit"—was positively related to creativity, originality, and effective leadership, whereas dysfunctional, disempowering self-talk—e.g., "You are always late. Good luck changing that behavior"—was negatively related to the same categories.

Constructive self-talk, or what I will call your "inner Jedi" (picture Yoda from the Star Wars movies), doesn't deny negativity, difficulty, or struggle—but chooses to confront them with calmness and confidence. Your inner Jedi is motivated by empathy, curiosity, creativity, passion, and purpose. When you tap into your inner Jedi, you lead with more happiness and hope, which facilitates more success in your work and relationships and leads you to higher performance. Your inner Jedi sounds like this:

- "I am the best leader for my team."

- "The work I do will help millions of people."

- "I am a problem solver and can figure out anything that comes my way."

- "Yes, that was disappointing, but we can learn and do it differently next time."

This type of constructive, inner-Jedi self-talk has been found to do the following:

- Reduce work stress.

- Lead to higher job satisfaction.

- Enhance the ability to attract followers as a leader.

- Facilitate a productive work environment and culture.

Conversely, destructive, dysfunctional self-talk, or what I will call your "inner Darth Vader" (yeah, I know he's part of the Sith) *thrives* on negativity, difficulty, and struggle, and it leads you to sabotage your own success. When you allow yourself to be influenced by your inner Darth Vader, you are focused on fear, stress, anger, guilt, shame, and judgment. Your inner Darth Vader sounds like this:

- "That's impossible."

- "I am a terrible leader and can never do anything right."

- "There is no way we can get this done on time."

- "Whenever we try a new product or a new way of doing things, it never works."

This type of destructive, dysfunctional self-talk has been found to do the following:

- Undermine self-efficacy, or one's belief in their ability to perform tasks.

- Lead to fixation on negative aspects of oneself or their job, which limits their ability to think broadly.

- Lead to seeing problems as obstacles (instead of opportunities).

- Decrease one's ability to be persistent.

We developed our thought patterns early in life, and your inner Darth Vader was developed to protect you from harm. By the time you are an adult, you don't need these thought patterns in the same way. Many times, instead of protecting you from harm, they sabotage your success, get in the way of your fullest potential, and don't allow you to reach your life's purpose. What's freeing to know is these thought patterns are habitual and automatic, which

GET GRITTY

GET PURPOSE

MASTER THOUGHTS

KNOW SELF

DOMINATE CONTROLLABLES

OWN THE MOMENT

CHOOSE EMOTIONS

OWN WHO YOU ARE

LIVE AND LET GO

COURAGE ZONE

means you can retrain your mind to think more on purpose about yourself and your situation through daily mental conditioning. When you do, you stay gritty and lead more effectively. You develop new neural pathways, and your thought patterns change, gaining new awareness and intention. In one study published in the *Journal of Organizational Behavior*, for example, business employees who received mindset training experienced increased mental performance, self-efficacy, enthusiasm, job satisfaction, and optimism about the organization as well as decreased nervousness.

We need strategies in our mental toolbox that we can use daily to channel our inner Jedi. Using mindset strategies each day to master our thoughts has been found to help entrepreneurs have a more optimistic outlook on future business challenges. Here are some thought strategies you can use as an entrepreneur, salesperson, or business leader to channel your inner Jedi more often, a few of which I expand on at the end of the chapter:

- **Reframe stressful events as learning experiences** – Negative events and obstacles help you learn more about yourself, your situation, what is important to you, and your desire to reach your goals. Ask yourself, *What's the opportunity?*

- **Use positive self-talk and mental imagery to replace negative thoughts with positive beliefs and expectations** – Many of our thoughts are false and limit us. Instead, when you notice yourself thinking in a disempowering way, ask yourself, *What is a thought that would serve me better right now?*

- **Actively find and imitate positive role models** – Author and motivational speaker Jim Rohn said, "You are the average of the five people you spend the most time with." Ask yourself, *Who is in my corner that I could model?*

- **Regularly observe your behavior through journaling** – Journaling just fifteen minutes a day, three to five times a week has been found to improve your physical and mental health. Journaling can also help your injuries heal faster (wow, huh!), and improve your problem-solving skills. Ask yourself, *How could I journal regularly to process what is going on in my head?*

- **Use techniques that increase mental and physical relaxation** – Relaxation techniques reduce stress and muscle tension and calm brain activity. Ask yourself, *How can I spend time practicing relaxation regularly?*

- **Envision ways to successfully accomplish your goals and deal with obstacles that might get in your way** – Imagery is a powerful mental tool because your mind does not know the difference between a vividly imagined event and a real event. Think about potential obstacles, and imagine yourself crushing them. Ask yourself, *What do I want to imagine today?*

- **Be mindful that certain circumstances can trigger your negative emotions and thoughts** – Notice your thoughts and emotions from an observer's perspective, and remember you can choose a different point of view. Ask yourself, *What activates my negativity, frustration, and anger?*

These mental strategies allow you to remain optimistic and see business situations with a clear lens. Channeling your inner Jedi allows you to see different solutions and opportunities than if were letting your inner Darth Vader run the show. The future of your business is directly tied to your expectations and ability to see opportunity in difficulty. Research conducted by Martin Seligman, a professor at the University of Pennsylvania, suggested that leaders, entrepreneurs, and athletes who practice optimism are more likely to experience the following:

GET GRITTY

GET PURPOSE

MASTER THOUGHTS

KNOW SELF

DOMINATE CONTROLLABLES

OWN THE MOMENT

CHOOSE EMOTIONS

OWN WHO YOU ARE

LIVE AND LET GO

COURAGE ZONE

- **Longer life** – Optimists live longer than pessimists. Optimists experience fewer infectious diseases, are less likely to have cancer, and have overall better health habits than pessimists.

- **Better, consistent performance** – Optimists perform better under pressure and have more consistent results than pessimists.

- **Less stress and more self-confidence and resilience** – Optimism decreases the bad and increases the good.

- **Improved persistence and commitment** – Optimists stay committed to their goals in the face of setbacks and uncertainty, focusing on the good in any given situation.

- **Deeper and lasting relationships** – Optimists have a stronger ability to influence others and to develop extensive networks.

These are powerful benefits of choosing an optimistic perspective, and they provide a strong rationale for why we should choose powerful self-talk.

What's Negativity Got to Do with It?

I think most entrepreneurs, salespeople, and business leaders know they should talk to themselves powerfully and lead with optimism. But that is easier said than practiced. You may be wondering, *What role does negativity play in all of this, and why do we experience it?* As humans, we have a negativity bias. We pay attention to negative information more often than positive information. In fact, we seek out negativity. Our negativity bias keeps us safe, yet it can prevent us from leading ourselves and others, forming relationships, and taking risks in the pursuit of building our businesses.

Our negativity bias is evolutionary in nature, a remnant from our hunter-gatherer ancestors. At some point, they had to fight animals to stay alive. It was life or death. In fact, our brains are mostly wired to keep us safe, not necessarily to help us stay gritty, perform consistently, or build our dream businesses. We inherited genes that predispose us to give special attention to the negative; your amygdala—the almond-shaped mass of gray matter in your brain that is associated with emotions—uses about two-thirds of its neurons to look for bad news. Rick Hanson, PhD, describes our mind as being like Velcro for negative experiences and like Teflon for positive experiences. It's biased toward negative experiences. He also calls the amygdala the "alarm bell of your brain," and that is because of the following two phenomena:

1. **Negative experiences are quickly stored in our memory** – In fact, for our brains to store positive memories long-term, we typically need to hold them in our awareness for a dozen or more seconds. I call this the "12-Second Rule."

2. **Negative memories linger longer than positive memories** – We are more likely to remember that potential client that said no over the one that said yes, turning into our most profitable client.

I've been using the 12-Second Rule—holding a positive event in your awareness for a dozen or more seconds—often lately, to combat the negativity in the world. For example, I've been savoring the smaller positive experiences I previously took for granted (e.g., the good-morning smile from one of my boys or my husband) as well as the larger positive experiences that might have otherwise been stored as mere events (e.g., a coaching client lauding the power of our work together, or several appreciative emails received after a I crushed a keynote).

GET GRITTY

GET PURPOSE

MASTER THOUGHTS

KNOW SELF

DOMINATE CONTROLLABLES

OWN THE MOMENT

CHOOSE EMOTIONS

OWN WHO YOU ARE

LIVE AND LET GO

COURAGE ZONE

One instance of using the 12-Second Rule had a profound impact on me: At the beginning of the COVID-19 pandemic, when my family was in lockdown in our home and there was so much fear and uncertainty in the word, I used the 12-Second Rule one night, when we were all playing hide-and-go-seek in the dark (my two boys are twelve and fourteen). I sat in the dark and just savored the moment. I took in the positivity for at least twelve seconds, moving the moment from my short-term memory to my long-term memory. I was grateful that my teenage boys still wanted to hang out with their parents in the dark! When I look back at that period, that moment, playing together in our basement—not the negative news or the fear we all felt—is one of the highlights, because I savored it. *Savoring* is actually a common term used in psychology. Savoring is noticing and appreciating the positive experiences in your life, and it helps you develop a long-lasting stream of positive emotions and thoughts—and it only takes twelve seconds, but go ahead and savor for longer, if you want.

We all experience negativity and have negative thoughts. One study found, however, that women are more likely to *internalize* negativity (e.g., depression or sadness), whereas men are more likely to *externalize* negativity (e.g., outward anger). How does negativity manifest in you? Are you more likely to internalize negativity or externalize it? Keep in mind that we cannot completely eliminate negativity—that should not be our goal, but we do need tools to combat negativity.

Let me make one thing clear: negative thoughts aren't always bad, especially while building a business. Negative thoughts can prevent us from making poor business decisions as well as help us not be overconfident in our own skills or those of our coworkers or employees. Yet, negative thoughts—disempowering, inner Darth Vader-type thoughts—more often hinder than help us in building and leading our business.

I like Daniel Amen's description of negative thoughts as "ANTs," or Automatic Negative Thoughts, which he wrote about in his book *Change Your Brain, Change Your Life*. This concept has helped me a lot in terms of building my own business. My negative thoughts, just like yours, are automatic. I don't always choose my thoughts, but I can decide how I respond to them—how I address negative thoughts that threaten to hold me back.

Some Common Automatic Negative Thoughts (ANTs)

- **"Always/Never" Thinking** – We tend to use words and phrases like *no one, everyone, every time, everything, never,* and *always,* out loud or in our mind (e.g., "Every time I reach out to that type of client, he/she always says no").

- **Focusing on the Negative in a Situation** – This happens when we see only the bad in a situation and not the good. This type of thinking doesn't give us the energy to tackle tough situations in our business or allow us to thrive.

- **Fortune-Telling** – When we fortune-tell, we can usually predict the worst possible outcome of a situation. Fortune-telling can help us plan, but if we focus on the worst possible outcome for too long, we experience a lack of energy, passion, and fulfillment.

- **Mind-Reading** – We mind-read when we believe we know what other people are thinking. In our heads, this may sound like *This client thinks this is bogus* or *They probably won't like what I post on social media.* Of course, we have no idea what other people are thinking unless we ask them.

GET GRITTY

GET PURPOSE

MASTER THOUGHTS

KNOW SELF

DOMINATE CONTROLLABLES

OWN THE MOMENT

CHOOSE EMOTIONS

OWN WHO YOU ARE

LIVE AND LET GO

COURAGE ZONE

- **Guilt-Tripping** – Guilt can result from using words and phrases like *should, must, have to,* and *ought to*. Guilt can be counterproductive because it creates a resistance to what we need to do.

- **Personalization** – We personalize when we believe negative events have personal meaning—we take events personally. The majority of the time, however, people are not thinking about us at all.

- **Labeling** – This happens when we attach a negative label to others or ourselves, saying things like "I am such a terrible leader" or "I am miserable at speaking in front of others." The problem with this is that we lump others or ourselves into categories and start generalizing, then start acting according to those generalizations.

- **Blaming** – This happens when you blame someone else for problems that pertain to you or your business. This is one of the most dangerous and poisonous ANTs—a fire ANT, so to speak. Blaming may sound like "It's your fault that . . ." or "This wouldn't have happened if . . ." When you blame others for your problem, you take away your power to solve it.

Talk to Yourself (Don't Just Listen)

As a business leader, it's essential that you don't believe everything you think, because your brain is there to keep you safe, watching for negativity. Noticing your ANTs is the first step in controlling your mind. You have a choice in how you address your ANTs. Awareness is the first step in controlling your mind—that is, listening to your mind nonjudgmentally and deciding which ANTs to believe and which are holding you back from your potential as a leader and person.

One thing is certain—your thoughts can level up your life and your business! To level up your business, you must first level up your thoughts about yourself and the possibilities that exist for your business. The single most important factor in your success is how you talk to yourself—about yourself and your experiences. We interpret each event that happens in our lives through our self-talk. We must watch the words we use to describe events externally and internally. Imagine that two business owners experience the same event in their business—say, an external, uncontrollable event such as the COVID-19 pandemic and a 20 percent decrease in sales during that time. One owner frames the event as devastating, evoking hysteria, which leads them to remain stuck in a mindset of fear and anxiety, not making adjustments to their business to serve their clients. The other business owner notes the uncontrollable nature of the event and looks for opportunities to adjust their offerings based on their clients' needs. They might describe the event as a time to live their mission and purpose to serve the world.

Everything in your life is based on the meaning you give it. We are meaning-making machines. *You* choose the meaning you give to a future event, and *you* choose the meaning you give to a past event that may play on repeat in your mind unconsciously. When you engage in daily mental conditioning, you consciously and proactively choose a meaning that empowers your future. You can see any situation—even a very difficult one—as happening *for* you, not *to* you. When you see something as happening *for* you, you learn from it. Seeing difficulties as opportunities helps you grow. Every circumstance can be turned into a gift. When you see problems as happening *to* you, you choose a victim mentality, taking it personally, perhaps wondering *Why me?* You stay stuck.

GET GRITTY

GET PURPOSE

MASTER THOUGHTS

KNOW SELF

DOMINATE CONTROLLABLES

OWN THE MOMENT

CHOOSE EMOTIONS

OWN WHO YOU ARE

LIVE AND LET GO

COURAGE ZONE

To help shift your perspective to seeing every difficulty as happening *for* you, not *to* you, consider this scenario: You lose a big client—the most profitable client you've ever had. Your first impulse is to beat yourself up, to judge yourself, which would likely lead you to lash out at your team. But instead, you choose to see the loss as a gift. You realize you could have cared for the client better and done a few things differently. As a result, you make changes in your business, which leads you to get ten more big clients just like the one you lost. Most of us don't want to think about difficulty—we are quick to avoid pain and move on. So we don't reflect or ask ourselves "How is this a gift? How is this happening *for* me?" But gritty high performers like you know the importance of positive energy and an empowering mindset.

Now ask yourself the following:

- What are the big things in my life that I want to give new meaning to, seeing them as happening *for* me?

- What are the events in my past that I want to give new meaning to, seeing them as having happened *for* me?

Next, consider:

- Choose a meaning that empowers you, not one that enables you.

- Choose a meaning that makes your better, not bitter.

- Choose a meaning that helps you, not one that hinders you.

- Choose a meaning that acknowledges that the events happened *for* you, not *to* you.

Great work! You're one step closer to having more grit, energy, and passion for your work and life.

Ample research over many decades has shown that the most successful businesspeople think differently than those who experience less success, because they look for the opportunity in difficulty. They see their struggles and difficulties as happening *for* them, not *to* them. They condition their minds to think big and believe in the impossible. They deliberately place energy, daily, into mastering the space between their ears. It's not automatic.

Daily mental conditioning takes two intentions: (1) starting your morning with powerful thoughts that prime your focus and (2) using tools throughout your day to shift your focus, address negativity, and train yourself to see the opportunities happening *for* you. Let's dive into the first way—starting your morning with powerful thoughts that prime your focus.

One way to condition yourself with powerful thinking is the GRIT Priming Exercise described earlier in this book. To help you condition your mind daily, let's dive deeper into the *T* section (Talk to Yourself with Power Phrases). In that section, I asked you to state, out loud or silently in your mind, 10–30 Power Phrases that reflect how you want to condition yourself to think. A Power Phrase is a statement that gives you power and reflects who you are or what you want to become—whereas you might otherwise just let your mind fixate on doubt and insecurity. The most powerful Power Phrases begin with "I am . . . ," a statement about your identity and who you are. The phrase "I am . . ." has the ability to shape your reality and your destiny. What you think about yourself is what you become. Therefore, you can train your mind to level up your belief in yourself and remember all that you already are. You just need to look inside. Ask yourself, *What do I need to believe about*

GET GRITTY

GET PURPOSE

MASTER THOUGHTS

KNOW SELF

DOMINATE CONTROLLABLES

OWN THE MOMENT

CHOOSE EMOTIONS

OWN WHO YOU ARE

LIVE AND LET GO

COURAGE ZONE

myself, my leadership, and my ability to reach my personal and business visions?

Here are a few of my clients' Power Phrases to give you some ideas:

- "I know my value and the value of my work to this world."

- "I am attracting leads that will deliver record earnings next quarter."

- "I am a pioneer who gives her life to serving others."

- "I show grace with myself and others daily."

- "I embrace and love who I am."

- "I am thriving right now and have enough business."

- "Every day and in every way, I am enough."

- "I own who I am."

- "I am compassionate and courageous with others."

- "I am fun, loving, confident, and imperfect."

- "Every day and in every way, I am grateful for this journey of life."

- "I know my financial foundation is secure and thriving."

- "I am experiencing my favorite year in business and have enough profits to satisfy my needs."

As you write your list in the exercise below, consider that the World's Best choose thoughts that help them stay focused on the possibilities. High performers don't hope their thinking will work for them; they *make* their thinking work for them. They are intentional and purposeful with their daily self-talk. They condition their minds each and every day. Don't let your thoughts happen by chance. Chance thinking does not lead to success. Intentional thinking does.

Exercise: Talk to Yourself

To gain clarity on the personal qualities you want to focus on improving, type or write out the 10–30 Power Phrases you want to say to yourself each morning. As you do so, consider using these powerful questions:

- What do I need to believe about myself, my leadership, and my ability to reach my personal and business visions?

- To level up my business, what do I need to believe about my value or the value I provide?

Here are the prompts I gave you in the introduction:

- "I am . . ."

- "Every day and in every way, I am . . ."

- "I take . . ."

- "I learn . . ."

- "I know . . ."

- "I show . . ."

- "Every day, I . . ."

Almost all of my clients do this GRIT Priming Exercise each morning. They tell me they are more positive, motivated, and intentional and that they show more patience with those they lead. Repeating these statements, either out loud or silently in your mind, each morning primes your subconscious, and the

GET GRITTY

GET PURPOSE

MASTER THOUGHTS

KNOW SELF

DOMINATE CONTROLLABLES

OWN THE MOMENT

CHOOSE EMOTIONS

OWN WHO YOU ARE

LIVE AND LET GO

COURAGE ZONE

statements will pop into your conscious mind when you need them the most—before a big presentation, before you give an employee tough feedback, or right before calling a client you would like to close.

Three Strategies to Level Up Your Thoughts

Besides a morning GRIT Priming Exercise, we also need to use mental tools throughout our day to shift our focus, address negativity, and train ourselves to see the opportunity despite the difficulty. Here are three strategies you can use to level up your thoughts during the day:

1. The Truth Meter – The Truth Meter involves asking yourself three quick questions when you notice that you are focusing on a disempowering thought. We want to notice the thought nonjudgmentally—no reason to judge yourself, as we all experience negativity and thoughts that are disempowering. And remember that the goal is not to eliminate all negative thoughts but to reduce the power they hold over you. Once your notice a negative thought, silently ask yourself the following:

> **a. Is this thought true?** – Your answer to this question may be yes or no. If it is no, remember that a thought is just a thought, nothing more. A thought is not a fact, and you don't need to believe it. Your mind is likely lying to you—remember, its role is to keep you safe, not help you think in a productive way.

> **b. Is this thought serving me?** – Your answer to this question is likely no. By "serving," I mean making you better, assisting you in reaching your potential, or helping you reach your vision. The thought is likely making you bitter, hindering you, or enabling you, or you might be taking the thought personally

and believing it. If the thought is not helpful or constructive, address it.

c. What is an empowering thought that _would_ serve me right now? – Choose an empowering thought to focus on, one that serves you and helps you reach your vision and potential.

Let's say, for example, you think to yourself, _There is no way we will reach our financial goals for Q4._ You know this thought is not true because there is still an opportunity to pivot and adjust. You also know it isn't serving you because you feel stuck and unable to think creatively to solve your problem. You decide to choose the following thought as your focus, because you believe it helps you step into your leadership and potential: _We will find a way to reach our financial goals for Q4 by continuing to innovate and try new strategies._ Focusing on this thought helps you and your team continue to pivot and adjust.

2. The Three OPP Strategy – When presented with a difficulty, this strategy asks you to identify three opportunities. The Three OPP Strategy helps you choose optimism and primes you to expect that something good will come from everything. Here is the process in a bit more detail:

a. First, think of a difficulty you are experiencing right now in your life or business. Maybe the market is down, or you aren't attracting the clients you desire, or you know you need to market more strategically but aren't sure how.

b. Second, consider at least three opportunities that come from this difficulty. Perhaps it provides an opportunity for you to learn new techniques to market

GET GRITTY

GET PURPOSE

MASTER THOUGHTS

KNOW SELF

DOMINATE CONTROLLABLES

OWN THE MOMENT

CHOOSE EMOTIONS

OWN WHO YOU ARE

LIVE AND LET GO

COURAGE ZONE

your business, to hire additional staff, or to be more creative during this period.

c. Finally, write the three opportunities down on paper or using a computer. How can you keep these opportunities in focus as you navigate this difficulty? Obstacles and setbacks are a given; it's how we respond to them that matters.

3. Reframing – Negative events and other obstacles help you learn more about yourself, your situation, what is important to you, and your desire to reach your vision and goals. The key is to shift your perspective to view each difficulty as an opportunity to grow and learn. Reframing helps you stay stoked and excited despite obstacles and hardships. Here are a few examples of when to reframe:

- A customer provides difficult feedback.

- You lose a big client or sale.

- The market negativity impacts your bottom line.

- You're in a cranky mood when you wake up.

The key is to step back and consider the frame, or "lens," of the situation. Don't ignore the difficulty or obstacle, but choose to see it from a different perspective. How can you challenge the thought, belief, or assumption underlying how you see the event? What is another way of looking at the event or situation with an alternative lens? How can you see this situation as a gift, happening *for* you, not *to* you?

My High Performance Game Plan
MASTER YOUR THOUGHTS

1. I commit to conditioning my mind each morning, using mindset tools throughout my day to think powerfully about myself and my business.

2. I commit to understanding my own negativity bias, nonjudgmentally noticing the ANTs holding me back from realizing my vision.

3. I will determine the 10–30 Power Phrases I will say to myself each morning, because what I think about myself, I become.

4. The next time I am faced with a difficulty, I will use the Three OPP Strategy, knowing that difficulties happen *for* me, not *to* me.

Now, take a moment to record the following on your Grit Board:

- Four to five of your Power Phrases

- Other instructive phrases such as "Use the Truth Meter," "See the opportunity," and "Talk to yourself (don't just listen)."

My High Performance Power Phrase:

I talk to myself—I don't just listen. I see the opportunity in every difficulty.

4

Know Yourself to Master Yourself

SUCCESS

What people think it looks like · What it really looks like

The World's Best

understand themselves and their tendencies, and they are in tune with their thoughts, emotions, and actions. They know they need to master themselves to be successful.

Chapter 4

Know Yourself to Master Yourself

"Learn to know yourself . . . to search realistically and regularly the processes of your own mind and feelings."
—NELSON MANDELA, FORMER PRESIDENT OF SOUTH AFRICA

I met Ron "RJ" Vetter, the CEO of Vetter Stone and Alabama Stone, several years ago, and we hit it off right away. I loved his positive energy. We had lunch and connected. Later, when I was thinking about the concept of knowing yourself to master yourself, I instantly thought of him. He'd seemed confident and comfortable in his own skin from the moment I met him. Ron has led Vetter Stone and Alabama Stone (the former acquired the latter) for about twenty years, and together the companies are known for their consistently high-quality stone, technical precision, and personalized service. It all started with his grandfather's vision and philosophy, which still drives the company today.

At age sixty-five, Paul Vetter Sr. was nearing retirement and running a small custom shop, and he wanted to start a larger company for his boys. He brought the idea to his wife, who was well educated, with six master's degrees. She responded, "Paul, this is your dream, and that's exactly what we're going to do." All his competitors told him he was making a mistake by using his life savings to start a stone company. They thought he couldn't compete against them because they were too big. Fun fact: today, all those competitors but one are nonexistent—they all either closed or Vetter Stone bought them out.

Ron's grandfather was involved in the company for many years before he died, leaving his youngest son, Howard (Ron's father), to run the company. In my interview with him, Ron said, "He would be proud to know that we have helped build high-rise towers in California and New York, and it would blow his mind to know we are doing work in China, Japan, and the Middle East." When asked about his grandfather's philosophy, Ron said it was that "whoever you're working with at any given moment is your most important customer. [My grandfather] would give his customers his all."

When Ron's father was ready to give up day-to-day leadership of the business, they hired a consultant to help them decide if Ron or one of his siblings had what it would take to run the company. After years of decision-making, the family picked Ron. "You always need to take calculated risks in business," Ron said, "but one of the biggest mistakes I made personally at the beginning was related to my emotions. We were in a board meeting as a family, and our family consultant was there. I was more vocal than usual and going off with my emotions. I can't even remember what I was so passionate about." The family consultant asked Ron if he would drive her back to the hotel after the meeting. She told him, "You can't do that again. From this moment on, you only get to *respond*—never *react* again." Ron said he knew the difference between responding and reacting immediately. "It's the best advice I have ever learned from anyone," he said, "including in my undergraduate and graduate education."

As a leader, you can train yourself to respond, not react. Reacting is an "emotional purge," as Ron described it. When you *react*,

GET GRITTY

GET PURPOSE

MASTER THOUGHTS

KNOW SELF

DOMINATE CONTROLLABLES

OWN THE MOMENT

CHOOSE EMOTIONS

OWN WHO YOU ARE

LIVE AND LET GO

COURAGE ZONE

there is backpedaling to do. Whereas when you *respond*, you are deciding what you want to say and how you want to act, with purpose and intention. You prioritize data over emotions and get to know yourself at a deeper level. Even if you are called into a meeting or situation where you aren't sure how to respond, you could, as Ron suggested, "tell your people that you want to collect your thoughts on this and pick up the conversation tomorrow." This choice to respond, not react, has been key in helping Ron make intentional decisions about hiring and firing the right people, and it has helped deepen his leadership.

Self-awareness is having a deep understanding of yourself—your emotions, strengths, limitations, values, motives, and inner dialogue—and it is the foundation of intentional leadership, facilitating a clear vision for your life and business. Being self-aware requires self-reflection, thoughtfulness, and an understanding of how you impact others. And when you have high self-awareness, you are able to notice yourself, adapt your behavior to relate to others, and separate your responses from the environment around you.

The Power of Self-Awareness in Growing Your Business

Self-awareness—the first step in leading yourself—has become the latest buzzword in business, and for a good reason. Research suggests that when we see ourselves clearly, it helps us be more confident and creative, communicate more effectively, build stronger relationships, and have trusting relationships with others. Bestselling author Stephen R. Covey, author of *The 8th Habit*, wrote that self-awareness is necessary to discovering your voice and understanding that you have the freedom to consciously choose your responses in life and in business. Furthermore, self-awareness has been described as crucial when one is learning how to become a better leader, and it was rated "as the most

GET
GRITTY

GET
PURPOSE

MASTER
THOUGHTS

KNOW
SELF

DOMINATE
CONTROLLABLES

OWN THE
MOMENT

CHOOSE
EMOTIONS

OWN WHO
YOU ARE

LIVE AND
LET GO

COURAGE
ZONE

important capability for leaders to develop," according to a survey given to members of the Stanford Graduate School of Business Advisory Council—and they are not alone in that belief. Even though most people *believe* they are self-aware, research suggests that only 10–15 percent of people actually are. Surprising, huh?

Self-awareness has also been found to predict leadership effectiveness, so it stands to reason that self-awareness is key to being an authentic leader. Authentic leaders (which we will discuss in chapter 8) are able to accept themselves for who they are and remain true to themselves—an ability which starts with self-awareness. In addition, research has shown that leaders who are aware of their own emotions and can recognize their impact on others are more likely to be rated as effective leaders.

When you have high self-awareness, you are able to do the following:

- Notice your own emotions and respond intentionally

- Recognize and admit mistakes

- Better meet the goals and objectives of your organization

- Be objective with yourself and the situations you encounter

- Practice self-control and command over yourself

- See a situation from an outside perspective

- Work creatively and productively

- Make effective decisions

- Maintain your self-confidence despite adversity or setbacks

The above list is not exhaustive, but it does make a compelling case for business leaders to work on improving their self-awareness.

Self-awareness is also the foundation of emotional intelligence, which has been found—by author and science journalist Daniel Goleman as well as others—to be a better predictor of success in life and business than intellectual intelligence (IQ). Goleman defines *emotional intelligence* as "a person's ability to manage [their] feelings so that those feelings are expressed appropriately and effectively." It is the ability to speak the language of those that you serve and lead, as well as to recognize, understand, and manage your own emotions. Learning self-awareness is the first step in developing your emotional intelligence. Bottom line: understanding ourselves is at the heart of our performance as entrepreneurs, salespeople, and business leaders. In fact, high performance starts with self-awareness.

Your Brain, Hijacked

As we consider increasing our self-awareness and ability to lead ourselves first, it's helpful to know that we are working against our brain's natural tendencies. Your brain's main purpose is to ensure survival and self-preservation. Consider this: at one point, humans were fighting animals to stay alive. That dynamic is part of our fight-or-flight response, an automatic response to danger that allows us to react quickly without thinking.

Think of the last time you "lost it." Maybe you blew up at someone— your child, parent, or partner, perhaps while you were driving. Once you took a breath and stepped back from the situation, you knew you overreacted in the moment. This overreaction is your "amygdala hijacked," a phrase popularized by Daniel Goleman in his book *Emotional Intelligence: Why It Can Matter More Than IQ*, referring to an immediate and intense emotional reaction that is out of proportion to the current situation.

As mentioned in the previous chapter, your amygdala is an almond-shaped cluster near the back of your brain, above your brainstem, which processes your emotions. When you "lose it," it means your amygdala was instantly hijacked, triggering a reaction that occurred before your neocortex, the thinking part of your brain, could activate, analyze the situation, and come to a decision. In the driver's seat, so to speak, your amygdala interpreted the situation or stimuli and added its own spin, triggering an automatic reaction in your emotions and behaviors. What usually follows is the feeling that you aren't sure what just came over you. According to Rick Hanson, a psychologist and New York Times bestselling author, research has shown that differences in the activation of the amygdala "probably account for much of the variation, among people, in emotional temperaments and reactions to negative information." The tricky thing is that we need our amygdala to feel our feelings and develop relationships. Fortunately, you can train your brain and improve your ability to prevent, or even stop, an amygdala hijack.

The Space Between

In his bestselling book *Man's Search for Meaning*, Viktor Frankl, a neurologist and psychiatrist, described his experiences as an inmate in a concentration camp during the Holocaust. He and his family were subjected to the most brutal, unimaginable conditions; every minute presented ample opportunity for an amygdala hijack. He lost his entire family and he, himself, barely survived, yet he was able to develop his philosophy. "Between stimulus and response there is a space," he writes. "In that space is our freedom and power to choose our response. In our response lies our growth and freedom." To reduce amygdala hijacking and ultimately increase our self-awareness, we need to notice and expand the space between stimulus and response. In that space, we can choose how to respond, and that is how we grow. That space is where

GET GRITTY

GET PURPOSE

MASTER THOUGHTS

KNOW SELF

DOMINATE CONTROLLABLES

OWN THE MOMENT

CHOOSE EMOTIONS

OWN WHO YOU ARE

LIVE AND LET GO

COURAGE ZONE

we can find inner happiness, fulfillment, and control over our reactions—where we can decide to respond, not react.

One way to create that space is to increase your self-awareness and emotional intelligence. But you also need a strategy to use in the moment to gain control of your response when you feel frustrated, angry, or disappointed. You can prevent, or even stop, an amygdala hijack by pausing to think, then deciding to respond, not react. This allows your neocortex to activate, so you can choose the best and appropriate way to respond to the situation. I like to use a three-step process that I call Pause, Consider, Respond (PCR), which involves tapping into the natural processes within your body and giving yourself time to respond. Let's go over those in more detail.

Pause: Take a moment to pause and take a breath. Who is involved? What is the situation? If you have time, take a Power Breath: Breathe in slowly through your nose for six seconds, hold for two seconds, then breathe out slowly through your mouth for seven seconds—fifteen seconds total. Count silently in your head, and focus on your breathing. This brings energy to the front part of your brain, the neocortex, and it will help prevent an amygdala hijack.

Consider: Next, intentionally create space between the stimulus and your response by considering the context and possible outcomes. It can help to ask yourself reflection questions. Here are some examples:

- How do I want to respond right now?

- What personal values can guide me at this moment?

- How can I grow (not just *get*) through this?

- How can I acknowledge the person and the situation in a way that reflects my values?

Your answers should help you determine how you actually feel and where you want to apply your focus.

Respond: The last step is to choose your response with purpose and intention. What do you want to do? How do you want to do it? How do you want to feel during? Will you actively engage or provide passive support? Based on this particular situation, what will you choose?

When we create and hold space, we are less likely to have our buttons pressed. We take control of ourselves, creating choice. We are able to lead intentionally, including the hardest person to lead—ourselves.

A quick example: You've been working on closing a deal for six months, having presented to the decision makers multiple times. Your heart and soul is in the deal, and closing it would generate half of your revenue goal for the year—in one project. At the last minute, the president overrules the other decision makers and decides to go with a competitor. You can either react or respond:

- **Reaction:** You immediately react with anger, beating yourself up for the failure. That night, you come home frustrated. You see the dirty dishes in the sink, and your son comes down the stairs and says, "We never have anything good for dinner." Your amygdala gets hijacked, and you blow up at your son for not appreciating all you do for him, with the rest of your family watching. You see the shock on everyone's faces, and suddenly, you realize you have no idea what came over you.

- **Response:** Immediately after hearing the disappointing news, you use the PCR Strategy to prevent an amygdala hijack: You *pause*, giving yourself time to take some Power Breaths and to think about who and what

GET GRITTY
GET PURPOSE
MASTER THOUGHTS
KNOW SELF
DOMINATE CONTROLLABLES
OWN THE MOMENT
CHOOSE EMOTIONS
OWN WHO YOU ARE
LIVE AND LET GO
COURAGE ZONE

are involved. You *consider* and reflect on the relevant details—you're happy with your presentations, you like working with that type of client, you could have created a stronger relationship with the president, etc. Then you *respond* with intention and purpose, resolving to do better next time. Yes, you still come home disappointed that night, but you prevented a hijack, so you're able to be present with your family. By using the PCR Strategy, you led yourself intentionally, increasing both your emotional intelligence and self-awareness.

Now consider your answers to the following questions to reflect on when creating space is important to your own personal and business growth:

- What pushes your buttons, making it difficult for you to respond instead of react? What are your triggers? Consider both personal and professional scenarios. How can you use the PCR Strategy to prevent an amygdala hijack in those familiar situations?

- Name two to three times in the coming weeks where you want to make sure you respond, not react, in your business. How could you use the PCR Strategy to respond in those situations?

Having answered those questions, you should be able to move forward living your purpose more fully and intentionally.

Three Exercises to Increase Your Self-Awareness

In my work leading workshops with companies as well as coaching elite athletes, entrepreneurs, leaders, and salespeople one-on-one, we engage in a variety of exercises to increase self-awareness, including completing objective measures of self-awareness and emotional intelligence. Here are three exercises I commonly use:

1. Finding Your Best Self
2. Finding Your Flow
3. Finding Your Intentional Self-Leader

It is certainly fun to do these exercises in a group setting—to share, discuss, and see one another's reactions—but doing them by yourself is still incredibly helpful. Now let's cover each exercise in more detail.

1. Finding Your Best Self

Being at your best consistently is personally rewarding. When you are at your best, you are giving your life and business your all, and you have no regrets. Let's get more clarity on what your best looks and feels like.

Try to remember your best day at work ever. Did you close a big deal? Did you celebrate the success of a colleague? Were you recognized for your work? Whatever it was, hold it in your mind, and respond to the following prompts:

1. Describe your best day at work.
2. How were you feeling on your best day?
3. What actions led to your best day?
4. What thoughts led to your best day?
5. How did you respond, not react?
6. What specific actions could you take to replicate your best day (things within your control)?

Spend a bit more time reflecting on the last question than you

GET GRITTY

GET PURPOSE

MASTER THOUGHTS

KNOW SELF

DOMINATE CONTROLLABLES

OWN THE MOMENT

CHOOSE EMOTIONS

OWN WHO YOU ARE

LIVE AND LET GO

COURAGE ZONE

did on the others. Then commit to one or two actions you could take *today* to move the needle in your life and business, and do them.

Ask yourself the same question each day—what are one or two actions I can commit to *today* to move the needle forward in my life and business? You'll find this question to be a game changer and life changer!

Doing this exercise by yourself allows you to gain clarity on your best and what led to it. Once you are more clear on what your best looks and feels like, lead the same exercise with your team. If there are enough people, have them pair up or form small groups and share their answers.

2. Finding Your Flow

One of the components of ikigai, the Japanese word that translates as "reason for being" (discussed in chapter 2), is to get clear on what you love to do. What do you enjoy doing so much that you forget about your worries? What are you doing when "time flies"? Chances are that when you are doing it, you are experiencing *flow*, a term first coined by psychologist Mihaly Csikszentmihalyi, author of the bestselling book *Flow: The Psychology of Optimal Experience*. Csikszentmihalyi discovered—in his years of research on creativity and performance with a wide range of professionals, including Nobel Prize winners—that the secret to the optimal performance of successful people is their ability to reach a flow state—the ultimate optimal experience, when you are completely absorbed in an activity you enjoy. It feels effortless. And research shows that when you experience flow, you are more likely to be satisfied with your work and can better maintain energy, which is necessary when growing your business.

If you'd like to experience flow more often, here are a few things you can do:

- *Choose an activity that is challenging, but not too challenging –* According to Steven Kotler, author of *The Rise of Superman: Decoding the Science of Ultimate Human Performance*, the activity you choose should be about 4 percent beyond your skill level in order to keep your attention, so your brain releases neurochemicals such as dopamine. In other words, challenging yourself a little by moving slightly out of your comfort zone leads to flow.

- *Set a clear goal, but focus on the process –* Knowing what you want is important to experiencing flow. Think of something you are sure you want—but not something you feel obligated to do. Once you are clear on your objective, focus on the next step in the process of getting to your goal. Olympic and elite athletes know this best: when they think about winning, scoring, or getting first place, their performance quickly declines. Stay focused on the process in the present moment, and flow will be more likely to happen.

- *Concentrate on one task –* You cannot live up to your potential if your cannot focus. You may think that "multitasking" is efficient, but it is impossible to fully focus on two things at once. Dividing your attention makes flow impossible, as your productivity can decrease by as much as 60 percent. Csikszentmihalyi said that for us to experience flow, we need to (1) be in a distraction-free environment and (2) have control over what we are doing at all times.

On episode 359 of the *High Performance Mindset* podcast, I interviewed Dr. Sue Jackson, the psychologist who collaborated with Csikszentmihalyi to write *Flow in Sports: The Keys to Optimal Experiences and Performances.* Jackson gave incredible additional insight on how to tap into flow, suggesting that mindfulness is the key pathway (more about that in chapter 6).

GET GRITTY

GET PURPOSE

MASTER THOUGHTS

KNOW SELF

DOMINATE CONTROLLABLES

OWN THE MOMENT

CHOOSE EMOTIONS

OWN WHO YOU ARE

LIVE AND LET GO

COURAGE ZONE

She also shared three inhibitors to the flow experience, which we'll call The Three Fs:

1. Focusing on the outcome
2. Forcing flow
3. Focusing on yourself

When we focus on the outcome, we take our attention off the present moment and the process. When we force flow, we get further away from it, pressing and pushing instead of letting it come naturally. And when we focus on ourselves, we forget the reason we are doing the work—likely for someone else—which can lead to overthinking and feeling self-conscious.

So, let's think about what leads to flow for *you*. Think about a time that you were in flow. What did your flow zone feel like? What led to that feeling? Now write down all the activities in your life where you experience flow. Maybe it happens when you are preparing for a presentation, working on your marketing, or selling to a potential client. (As an example, I experience flow the most often when I am writing, speaking, and working one-on-one with my clients.) What do these activities have in common? Why do these particular activities lead to flow for you? Flow is like a muscle—the more you train and experience flow, the easier it will be to reach your flow zone and live according to ikigai.

3. Finding Your Intentional Self-Leader

In the first conversation I have with a one-on-one coaching client, we usually discuss the concept of leading intentionally. When you consider how you want to lead yourself, you become more aware of your influence, your position, your strengths, and the areas in which you want to improve. As John Maxwell said, "Leadership is influence—nothing more, nothing less. When you become a student of leaders, as I am, you recognize people's level of influence in everyday situations all around you."

Research shows that intentional leaders possess deep knowledge about themselves and recognize their strengths and the areas in which they could improve (aka self-awareness). They understand how they want to show up each day, and they follow their own direction in pursuit of their vision. Intentional leadership is the process of deciding how you want to be perceived and remembered by those you lead and then taking action to lead the way you intend.

The first step in intentional leadership is to define what it means to you and get clear on your priorities for yourself. Below are five questions to help you think about your intentions as a leader:

- What does it mean to you to be an intentional leader?

- Which values do you want to drive your leadership decisions?

- How do you want to be described by those you lead?

- When you are gone, what do you want people to say about you?

- What do you need to do each day to show up as an intentional leader?

After answering and reflecting on the five questions above, identify the gaps between how you want to lead and how you lead currently. How is your vision for your leadership different than the ways you currently lead? What do you need to change to be the leader you want to be? Commit to closing the gaps by using the tools presented in this book.

GET GRITTY

GET PURPOSE

MASTER THOUGHTS

KNOW SELF

DOMINATE CONTROLLABLES

OWN THE MOMENT

CHOOSE EMOTIONS

OWN WHO YOU ARE

LIVE AND LET GO

COURAGE ZONE

My High Performance Game Plan
KNOW YOURSELF TO MASTER YOURSELF

1. I commit to leading the most difficult person first, myself, by increasing the space between stimulus and response—today.

2. I will complete the Best Possible Self exercise to understand my best, and then I will replicate my best day by focusing on 1–2 commitments I can make—daily.

3. I'll spend some time this week thinking about times I experienced flow, then identify how I can experience flow more often.

4. I commit to being an intentional leader, showing up each day based on my values and how I want to be remembered.

Now, take a moment to record the following on your Grit Board:

- A short description of your insights from the Best Possible Self exercise

- A list of the ways you can lead intentionally

- Short, inspirational sentences such as "Respond, don't react"; "Lead myself"; and "Find my flow."

My High Performance Power Phrase:
**I choose to lead the hardest person first—myself.
I choose to respond with purpose and intention.**

Dominate the Controllables

The World's Best

dominate what they have control over—their APE— instead of what they cannot control.

Chapter 5

Dominate the Controllables

"When something I can't control happens, I ask myself: Where is the hidden gift? Where is the positive in this?"
—SARA BLAKELY, FOUNDER OF SPANX

I learned the importance of dominating the controllables about thirteen years ago, when my oldest son, Carter, was born and my family and I moved to Minnesota. As we were starting a family, my husband and I desired to be closer to our parents and siblings in Iowa and Nebraska, respectively. So we packed up our home in North Carolina, and the three of us hit the road. I had accepted a faculty position as a professor at Minnesota State University, Mankato. Moving across the country with a newborn, purchasing a house, starting a new job—that was a lot of big life changes in a two-month period. As I started my new job, there was talk of "retrenchment," which meant that the university was reducing costs and potentially laying off faculty. I wanted to learn more, so I decided to engage in one of the "water-cooler conversations" in the hallway—you know, the kind of conversations that are more about gossiping than solving problems. I started a conversation with Ted (or at least that's what we will call him). I asked Ted, "Who do you think will be laid off?" And he proceeded to say, "Cindra, I think it's going to be you!" He then listed what seemed like twenty reasons why he thought I would be laid off.

By the end of the conversation, I was convinced I was going to be cut, which made the next six months miserable for me. I didn't take good care of my newborn, myself, or my husband. I lacked energy and focus. I was a nervous wreck—a teacher just going through the motions, not focused on connecting with and serving my students. I complained a lot.

What Ted said to me that day was an *uncontrollable*—something we cannot personally control, such as what other people say and do. But I *could* control two things in that situation: (1) if I engaged in the conversation in the first place and/or (2) how I chose to respond to his comments. I could have arranged a meeting with the dean or president of the university to learn more about retrenchment and get information directly from those in charge. Instead, I made a story up in my mind. In that moment, I chose to react, not respond. I caused my own suffering.

I told this story for the first time about a year ago, during a keynote with high-level managers and salespeople, and sharing it made me feel vulnerable. But I wanted to share it to make the point that even the "expert" on developing the High Performance Mindset can get in her own way. Tina, who was in the audience, raised her hand and said, "This is MSU." *Minnesota State University*, I thought, smiling to myself, assuming she was referring to the university. "No," she said, "MSU means 'making shit up.'" The audience roared with laughter. She was right—I was making shit up.

That was a crucible moment for me (we'll talk about crucible moments in chapter 8); it was painful, and I felt like a victim, but I learned the importance of focusing on the controllables— and of not making shit up! I learned the importance of tracing information to its source, especially if you find yourself focusing on the uncontrollables out of anxiety or frustration. Knowing what's what goes a long way toward preventing burnout and ensuring you stay passionate and purposeful.

GET GRITTY

GET PURPOSE

MASTER THOUGHTS

KNOW SELF

DOMINATE CONTROLLABLES

OWN THE MOMENT

CHOOSE EMOTIONS

OWN WHO YOU ARE

LIVE AND LET GO

COURAGE ZONE

Dominating the Controllables

Dominating the controllables is an essential part of pushing yourself and your business forward, finding opportunity in difficulty, and continually adjusting your business to fit the needs of your clients. If you focus on what you cannot control, you are more likely to throw in the towel, close the doors of your business, let your amygdala get hijacked, and get stuck in an emotional rollercoaster.

Simply put, business can be divided into two areas: (1) things you *can* control and (2) things you *cannot* control. There are many things you cannot control in business: change, your competitors, the economy, regulations, the weather, advancing technology, pandemics, the economy, and your clients, not to mention other people's thoughts, actions, or perceptions that impact your operation.

I listed "change" first because it is the uncontrollable that I see people struggle with the most. As I wrote this chapter, we were in the middle of the COVID-19 pandemic, and the shelter-in-place order had just been lifted. Throughout this challenging time, I've witnessed fear and anxiety in people's faces and actions—I've felt it too. At the beginning of it all, as I read and heard bleak stories about the death toll and respirator shortages, I caught myself thinking, *Am I going to die alone?* There are many things we cannot personally control about COVID-19 (or any other pandemic, for that matter), including the decisions and behaviors of our government officials and fellow citizens as well as when (or if) things will open up.

When we focus on what we have no control over, we tend to experience frustration, anxiety, and fear, often trying to place blame. We let our amygdala get hijacked over and over and over again. These emotions, when experienced too often, can lead to stagnation, a lack of creativity and innovation, and the inability to pivot and adjust in times of transition and change. When we focus on the uncontrollables as leaders, our coworkers and employees are more likely to make excuses, feel powerless, and stay stuck, which drains our passion to lead. Every moment we spend focusing on things we cannot control is a lost opportunity to earn money. Staying focused on the uncontrollables negatively impacts our happiness and ability to continually develop our business in creative and innovative ways—we stop moving forward with our vision.

When we focus on what we *can* control, we are more likely to lead intentionally, stay excited and passionate, and choose empowering emotions, fueling us to tackle obstacles and challenges head-on. We can better handle the emotional rollercoaster that comes with entrepreneurship and business leadership, continually push the limits of our thinking, and have the grit to keep pushing. Focus on what you *can* control.

What Can We Actually Control?

What we can control boils down to the acronym APE, which I will explain below. When we are dominating our APE, we are showing up in the world—with our team and with our family— as the best version of ourselves. We don't let our attention go to things we cannot control; or if we do, we quickly refocus on what we *can* control. We are more likely to work hard toward our goals, stay gritty, and engage in thinking that contributes to business development. The acronym APE refers to three categories:

GET GRITTY

GET PURPOSE

MASTER THOUGHTS

KNOW SELF

DOMINATE CONTROLLABLES

OWN THE MOMENT

CHOOSE EMOTIONS

OWN WHO YOU ARE

LIVE AND LET GO

COURAGE ZONE

A – Attitude, Attention, and Actions

- **Attitude** – We control our attitude every minute of every day. Do a gut check: When you interact with your clients, coworkers, teammates, and family members, do you tend to put forth a more positive attitude, or a more negative attitude? Even in difficult circumstances, you can choose to see and focus on the good, to serve and give.

- **Attention** – Attention is like a mental spotlight. Imagine a miner or diver wearing a headlamp. Their attention is always on something; they're never really lost or blind. Is your attention straying from your dream, or is it laser focused on it? Are you easily distracted? At any given moment, you can choose to shine your attention on what helps you. Your attention determines how you feel.

- **Actions** – Our attitude and attention drive our actions. Are your daily actions driving you forward? Are you taking massive action each day and focusing on the "needle movers" in your business—the actions that directly drive results? Are you practicing self-care— eating, sleeping, and caring for yourself like a high performer?

P – Preparation, Passion, and Purpose

- **Preparation** – We are in complete control of our preparation. High performers dominate their process, in part by making sure they are prepared. We all have the same amount of time each day: 86,400 seconds. Is what you are doing with your 86,400 seconds moving you closer to your long-term goals, or further away?

- **Passion** – Passion is the energy that comes from focusing on what lights the fire in your belly. Passion needs to be cultivated; we can choose to focus on either what brings us energy or what drains our energy. What are you most passionate about? How have you—or can you—align your business with your passion? Does the way you spend your time each day support living your passion? Connecting with your passion is an ongoing process that is integral to living your best life and reaching your business vision.

- **Purpose** – Your purpose is what makes you unique. Purpose is fundamental to our health, happiness, and healing, and it is controllable. What makes you get out of bed in the morning? How is your purpose connected with your business? How can you connect with your purpose each day? Living your purpose is like driving your car with a full tank of gas.

E – Effort, Emotions, and Energy

- **Effort** – We completely control our effort. High performers don't just go through the motions; they choose full engagement and deliberately pursue their best each and every day, because they know what their best looks like. They are locked in to their goals and dreams. They keep going despite setbacks, challenges, uncontrollables, mistakes, disappointments, and heartbreaks. Are you putting in the level of effort needed to achieve your big goals and dreams? What's one thing you could do to put in the effort required?

GET GRITTY

GET PURPOSE

MASTER THOUGHTS

KNOW SELF

DOMINATE CONTROLLABLES

OWN THE MOMENT

CHOOSE EMOTIONS

OWN WHO YOU ARE

LIVE AND LET GO

COURAGE ZONE

- **Emotions** – Our emotions comprise clues and information that help us understand what is important to us. In her book, *Emotional Agility*, Susan David describes how we can label our feelings, then ask ourselves what led to us feeling that way; we can see our emotions through a lens of curiosity and compassion, knowing we can act independently of how we feel. Are your emotions helping you build your business, or are they hindering you? Do the emotions you experience daily allow you to be creative, innovative, and purposeful with your actions? What emotions do you want to feel more of?

- **Energy** – Consider a power plant. It doesn't have energy; it *generates* energy. You are similar. You generate energy with your thoughts and actions when you focus on gratitude, creativity, and your vision for the future. How do challenges and difficulties help you grow? Do disappointments happen *for* you, or *to* you? (I think you know the answer by now.) You can generate more positive energy by living each day with unfailing enthusiasm and clear purpose.

As you read this, you may think it seems easy enough to focus on your controllables and your APE. But for most people, including myself, it takes daily effort. As humans, our default is to focus on the uncontrollables. It is much easier to blame, complain, and make excuses than to take a close look in the mirror and examine ourselves and our actions.

Taking Full Responsibility for Everything

Taking full responsibility for everything you control is at the core of focusing on controllables. Full responsibility—100 percent—sounds extreme, I know. Taking full responsibility means knowing you are the one that produces the results in your life and business. You are responsible for the quality of your life, the relationships you build, and the business you grow. You are responsible for your actions, your guiding beliefs, the thoughts you accept as true, and the images you hold in your mind. You—and only you—are responsible for your success or lack thereof.

The most successful salespeople, entrepreneurs, and business leaders take full responsibility for their past and future; they know it was their choices that led them to where they are today. They see their vision clearly and grab ahold of it. They know they are in control of their destiny.

Taking full responsibility is difficult to practice. About two years ago, I attended a day-long training led by Jack Canfield. I loved his book *The Success Principles* and its companion workbook, so I was excited to participate. Within the first hour of the workshop, he talked about responsibility. I thought to myself, *I already take 100 percent responsibility. This is a fundamental concept in* Beyond Grit—*part of what I teach.* Then my eyes were opened.

Jack had us turn to someone we didn't know and answer the same prompt back and forth for three or four minutes: *If I were to take 5 percent more responsibility in my life, I would* . . . I almost couldn't believe what came out of my mouth—"I would eat healthier every day . . . run every day . . . have more patience with my boys . . . show my husband more love . . ." I thought—in my mind—that I'd already been taking 100 percent responsibility. But Jack's exercise helped me realize what taking full responsibility felt like—in my heart.

GET GRITTY

GET PURPOSE

MASTER THOUGHTS

KNOW SELF

DOMINATE CONTROLLABLES

OWN THE MOMENT

CHOOSE EMOTIONS

OWN WHO YOU ARE

LIVE AND LET GO

COURAGE ZONE

Consider what it would mean for *you* to take 100 percent responsibility. If you took 5 percent more responsibility than you're taking now, what would that look like? What part of your APE can you take 5 percent more responsibility for?

At the end of my day, I take the Responsibility Test. As I lie in bed, I ask myself, "Did I take 100 percent responsibility today?" If I answer no, I show myself some compassion, remembering that I am human (just like you) and that tomorrow is a new day. I wake up the next morning ready to take 100 percent responsibility.

How Do We Actually Dominate the Controllables?

Dominating the controllables takes daily effort and attention. Remember, humans do not naturally focus on what they can control. We need an easy tool to help us refocus. Use this super-short three-step process to dominate your attention on the controllables:

1. First, catch yourself in a compassionate, nonjudgmental way: notice, or note, that your attention is on something you cannot control. The sooner you notice, the sooner you can course correct. Try not to let yourself focus on an uncontrollable for more than one second.

2. Next, say a phrase that reminds you to stay focused on what you can control. You might tell yourself to "dominAPE," "APE-up," or "control the controllables." ("DominAPE" was suggested by one of my audience members who liked puns. I like it!)

3. Finally, redirect your attention to what you can control. Focus on dominating your APE—your attitude, attention, and actions; your preparation, passion, and purpose; and your effort, emotions, and energy. Ask yourself, "What can I control right now?" or, "How can I take 100 percent responsibility right now?"

When we are dominating our APE, we are showing up in the world, on our team, in our business, and with our family as the best version of ourselves. DominAPE!

Three Strategies to Dominate the Controllables

If the quick three-step process above works for you—great! But there's more. Here are three strategies you can use to level up your thoughts during the day and stay focused on the controllables:

Believe the best is yet to come – Part of leading yourself is taking an optimistic view of the future. I like to think of the Frank Sinatra lyrics "You ain't seen nothin' yet // The best is yet to come. . . ." (Can you hear the tune in your mind?) Believing the best is yet to come means that you dominate your attitude— as a leader, *you* are the first to see opportunity in difficulty. You see the silver lining, believing your business will be stronger and better because of the difficulty, struggle, or mistake. You believe that good events will continue and that your attitude and energy attract positive customers and employees to your business. You have a relentless optimism where you regularly visualize your business three, five, or maybe even ten years from now, when you'll confidently know you have reached your goals. You remind your employees and those supporting you and your business that they "ain't see nothin' yet," because great things are going to happen for you all!

Develop a contingency plan – A contingency plan helps you deal with the unexpected. Dan Gould (one of my mentors) and his colleagues conducted several research studies on Olympic athletes and coaches. They found that those who succeeded at the Olympics had a plan to deal with distractions as well as a contingency plan for what might get in the way of being their best. To develop your own contingency plan, first complete the

GET GRITTY

GET PURPOSE

MASTER THOUGHTS

KNOW SELF

DOMINATE CONTROLLABLES

OWN THE MOMENT

CHOOSE EMOTIONS

OWN WHO YOU ARE

LIVE AND LET GO

COURAGE ZONE

question *What if . . . ?* and then complete the statement *Then I will . . .* It is simple *and* powerful. It helps you get unstuck and overcome fear, so you can feel confident and courageous in the moment. Here are some examples to help you stay creative, excited, gritty, and passionate about your work:

- **What if** we do not increase our sales after our new advertising campaign? **Then I will** decide on a new medium to market in.

- **What if** we don't make as much revenue as we hoped this year? **Then I will** continue to innovate and find new outreach strategies.

- **What if** I lose this big client or potential big deal coming up? **Then I will** keep pressing on, knowing I am meant for more and that great things are coming my way.

- **What if** we have to close the business early because of a pandemic like COVID-19? **Then I will** design a new marketing effort to increase business on days we are open or continue to find new ways to serve our clients.

Don't take things personally – When you get feedback from a client, friend, or colleague, listen or read the feedback like a text message—focusing on *what it says*, not *what you think it means*. Consider the feedback objectively—don't take it personally—and think about what you can learn from it, how you can adjust and adapt. This helps you focus on the controllables using the attitude, attention, and emotions that you want to feel. In his book *The Four Agreements*, Don Miguel Ruiz writes, "Nothing people do is because of you. What others say and do is a projection of their own reality, their own dreams." What people say and the feedback they provide are projections of their world, not yours. When you take things personally, you act and think selfishly. You get frustrated, overreact, get offended, and hold grudges. You create conflicts that can impact your relationships long-term. Instead, consider what you can learn from the feedback and move on quickly, staying focused on what you can control. DominAPE!

GET
GRITTY

GET
PURPOSE

MASTER
THOUGHTS

KNOW
SELF

DOMINATE
CONTROLLABLES

OWN THE
MOMENT

CHOOSE
EMOTIONS

OWN WHO
YOU ARE

LIVE AND
LET GO

COURAGE
ZONE

My High Performance Game Plan
DOMINATE THE CONTROLLABLES

1. I commit to using an APE phrase daily—such as "dominAPE"—to help me focus on things I can control.

2. I consider the uncontrollables that I tend to focus on, so that I can tell when they take my focus off my best.

3. At the end of my day, I take the Responsibility Test. As I lie in bed, I ask myself, "Did I take 100 percent responsibility today?" If not, I commit to doing so tomorrow.

4. I dominate my attitude—believing the best is yet to come—by reminding my employees and those that support my business to have relentless optimism.

Now, take a moment to record the following on your Grit Board:

- Your APE phrase.

- A few key phrases such as "Take 100 percent responsibility," "Believe the best is yet to come," or "Don't take things personally."

My High Performance Power Phrase:

I dominate the controllables. I take 100 percent responsibility for my success.

Own the Moment

The World's Best

recognize that they can't control the past or future, and they are empowered to reach their highest potential when engaged in the present moment.

Chapter 6

Own the Moment

"The future depends on what we do in the present."
—MAHATMA GANDHI

Mark Watkins formed Geneva Capital, an equipment-financing company, in 2000. He started the company with his own money and quickly lost $35,000 in the first six months. It didn't look too promising to start, but Mark believed in his vision and his ability to implement it. He knew he needed more capital to make the company work, so he took a risk by taking out a second mortgage on his family's home. In our interview, he described the beginning of Geneva Capital as "very scary but exciting and invigorating all at the same time." He was on *the* entrepreneurial journey—dreaming big and taking risks, but focusing on the small steps to reach his big vision. When I asked Mark what kept him going during that time period, he said, "I had a family of four that fell on my shoulders. If I didn't make it happen, it wasn't going to happen. I had to believe that 'today is the day that great things will happen,' especially in the early years of building the business. The key is to always, always believe in yourself, or no one else will."

Geneva Capital is now the twenty-first largest equipment-financing company in the United States—with a $250 million portfolio and $120 million in new sales each year. The employees at Geneva Capital wouldn't have been able to serve their clients or build the company into what it is today without grit *and* the ability to own the moment. Mark continued to believe in his long-term goals, persevere by pivoting and adjusting his path, and choose courage and risk over comfort to reach his goals. He didn't give in to fear, anxiety, or pressure, even though the finances were tight when he started. Instead, he took it one day at a time, mastering the present moment.

When I asked Mark to share what grit means to him and how it helped him build the business to what it is today, he said, "Grit means achieving the goals you set out for yourself—you may need to go to plan B, plan C or plan D. There is no shame in that. Going to plan B, C, or D is not failure—that is success. That means you got out of your comfort zone. Sometimes you have to be willing to try new things and then focus on the small things, the daily tasks that will lead to success on a weekly or monthly basis." Mark is spot on here—as an entrepreneur, business leader, or salesperson, your success depends on keeping your goal and vision in mind while focusing on the present moment, pivoting and adjusting as necessary. Mark suggests we write out our plan B, C, and D so we can pivot and adjust accordingly. Having contingencies in place makes focusing on the present that much easier—and that's what owning the moment is all about.

In a study published in the journal *Science*, Harvard psychologists Matthew A. Killingsworth and Daniel T. Gilbert found that people spend about 47 percent of their waking hours thinking about something other than what they're doing. Wow! That's almost 50 percent of our day that we aren't thinking about what we are actually doing. Crazy! Focusing on things other than what we are doing typically makes us unhappy. The human mind wanders. We spend a lot of time thinking about what's going on around us, contemplating events that happened in the past, and imagining worst-case scenarios that may never happen. That, my friends, is our negativity bias and monkey mind—our mind

GET
GRITTY

GET
PURPOSE

MASTER
THOUGHTS

KNOW
SELF

DOMINATE
CONTROLLABLES

OWN THE
MOMENT

CHOOSE
EMOTIONS

OWN WHO
YOU ARE

LIVE AND
LET GO

COURAGE
ZONE

swings from thought to thought, like a monkey moving branch to branch. Killingsworth and Gilbert said that when predicting a person's unhappiness, the frequency with which their mind leaves the present is a better predictor than what they are doing. They write, "The ability to think about what is not happening is a cognitive achievement that comes at an emotional cost."

Even though the human mind tends to wander, the present moment is the *only* place our best performance can take place. It is where we experience flow and where we can be our best self as a leader, entrepreneur, or salesperson. Because of this natural tendency to focus on the future or past, we must train our mind to be in the present more often.

Your mind can be one of three places: the past, the present, or the future. When you are focused on the past, you can nurse grudges, recall instances where you were mistreated, and/or ruminate on past losses, failures, or rejections. Although thinking about yourself in the past can lead to *some* positive feelings, such as happiness and gratitude, it can also lead to a great deal of unnecessary suffering. We have to be conscious of how we think about the past so that we can give those events powerful meaning.

Past	Present	Future
Anger	Focused on the process in the present moment, you can do and be anything.	Fear
Frustration		Anxiety
Regret		Doubt
Depression		Pressure
Suffering		Results
		Outcome

Humans have a similar relationship with the future. We experience anxiety and fear when we think about all the things that could go wrong in our life or business, and the resulting pressure to avoid such events can hold us back from reaching our goals. And when we imagine our future self, we sometimes question and doubt if we can get there.

In comparison, thinking about the past and future can also lead to empowering emotions and actually motivate us. We can look back at our past and create meaning, seeing how events happened *for* us, not *to* us (see chapter 1). We can remind ourselves not to repeat past mistakes and even forecast how we might feel in the future, which helps guide us in the present. The key to high performance and being your best self is to stay more focused on the present moment than on the past or future, locked in on the small tasks you need to accomplish—the process.

Being Present with Your Process

When we are building our business and pushing forward, toward our vision of what's possible, it's easy to spend too much time thinking about and planning the future. This future-based thinking can motivate and excite us, but it can also lead to feelings of heaviness, pressure, gut-wrenching anxiety, and paralyzing fear. For example, I had a client that spent so much time thinking about his big, bold vision that his anxiety prevented him from making progress. His vision felt so big and far away, as if he would never reach it. I have found that the World's Best are able to choose when they focus on their vision and when they focus on the process, being strategic about where they apply their energy. They are able to tap into their vision for motivation and direction while staying focused on the daily tasks, or the process, that will build their business.

GET GRITTY

GET PURPOSE

MASTER THOUGHTS

KNOW SELF

DOMINATE CONTROLLABLES

OWN THE MOMENT

CHOOSE EMOTIONS

OWN WHO YOU ARE

LIVE AND LET GO

COURAGE ZONE

"The process" includes all the small things you need to do to reach your vision for your business and life. The process is what you do day in and day out to be successful. To get clear on your process, break down your goal and focus on what it takes to get there. This requires daily discipline as well as a focus on executing the fundamentals. Let's take the example of a financial planner who is building their business to reach their year-end goals. They have a chance to win a trip to Hawaii, funded by the corporate office, if they add seventy-five new clients this year. The seventy-five new clients and the trip are the outcome—the future-based goal. But what are the daily tasks they need to implement to reach that goal at the end of the year? That is the process. If they need a boost of motivation, they can focus on winning the Hawaii trip. But if they focus too much on the Hawaii trip, they might get frustrated with the process because the goal feels too far away. The habit of focusing on the process can be applied to any goal—increasing revenue, improving employee retention, launching a new division or product line, etc. To consider your process, do the following:

1. First, write down your goal(s) for the year. What do you desire and want this year? Choose 1–3 goals to write down. (More than three goals gives you too much to focus on.)

2. Next, outline the steps that are in your control to get there. What process do you need to follow to achieve extraordinary results? What are the daily tasks you need to complete to get it done?

It's important to stay focused on the daily process and the present moment, as it decreases stress, pressure, and anxiety. Plus, when you stay focused on the process, you are more likely to persist, stay passionate about your work, and have a higher sense of satisfaction. You'll also think less about failure and be more likely to try new things. You will choose to be courageous in the moment, which is essential to reaching your vision.

The Practice of Mindfulness

Too often, we let our amygdala get hijacked, reacting in ways that are inconsistent with our values and our vision for our business. Therefore, we need strategies for quieting our mental noise and bringing our attention to the present moment, ultimately reducing our suffering. We can train ourselves to focus on the present moment and our process. In that space, we can accomplish almost anything.

Practicing mindfulness and implementing mindfulness-based strategies can help quiet our inner chatter or trash talk in a nonjudgmental way, allowing us to focus on the present moment. As Jon Kabat-Zinn stated in his bestselling book *Full Catastrophe Living*, "Mindfulness means paying attention in a particular way, on purpose, in the present moment, nonjudgmentally." Mindfulness is being awake in the moment, fully paying attention to what is happening—both internally (noticing your thoughts and emotions) and externally (noticing what is going on around you with an open, curious, and nonjudgmental attitude). You are aware of what you are doing and where you are, without becoming overly reactive or overwhelmed.

The nonjudgmental component of mindfulness means paying attention to and observing your experiences instead of getting carried away with your quick reactions. You can respond, not react. When you are nonjudgmental as a leader, you can step back from your own experiences and observe your thoughts and emotions. The nonjudgmental component also means that you

GET GRITTY

GET PURPOSE

MASTER THOUGHTS

KNOW SELF

DOMINATE CONTROLLABLES

OWN THE MOMENT

CHOOSE EMOTIONS

OWN WHO YOU ARE

LIVE AND LET GO

COURAGE ZONE

work to accept what is and isn't working in your business. You don't fight or judge; instead, you notice and become aware.

The research on mindfulness and business suggests numerous benefits, including a real return on investment. Mindfulness has been found to . . .

- Boost your interpersonal skills and communication
- Lead to enhanced job performance
- Help you regulate emotions and maintain composure in tense situations
- Help you identify with emotions
- Help you detach from work
- Enhance your ability to get in the flow
- Lead to enhanced overall well-being
- Boost your ability to deal with stressful events
- Support self-confidence, creativity, and innovation
- Increase productivity and engagement of employees
- Help employees reduce their stress and risk of burnout

Given the numerous benefits mentioned above, mindfulness programs are popping up in many organizations, including Apple, Nike, General Mills, the US military, and major business schools. Even in Silicon Valley, companies such as Google, Twitter, and Facebook encourage their staff to practice mindfulness not just to have more inner peace but also to get ahead.

Earlier I mentioned that our mind is like a monkey in search of fruit in the forest, moving from one tree to another. Our mind can be restless, hard to control, and easily distracted and agitated.

I often notice my mind going from thought to thought to thought. How about you? That's why we need to practice mindfulness, and when we do, our mind can be calm and present.

Present-moment focus is about awareness first, then choice second.

At the heart of being mindful are two practices: awareness and choice. The first step is to notice and be aware of where your focus is. Second, choose to bring your attention to the present. Bringing your attention back to the present is a choice. It may not always be easy, but you can do it intentionally.

Ways to Practice Mindfulness

Below are a few ways you can practice mindfulness—anywhere, anytime, and with anyone. You can find additional resources on mindfulness, including a breathing exercise, at beyondgrit. com/bonus.

- Take five to fifteen minutes in the morning or during your day to quiet your mind. Take a seat and then notice your thoughts, feelings, and body. Feel your breath. When you notice your mind wandering, be kind to yourself. Don't judge—just come back to the present.

- Take a slow, mindful walk at lunch or during a break at work. Listen to what your body and mind might be trying to tell you. Notice your breath, your pulse, and your emotions.

- When you sit down for a new meeting, notice the surroundings and take in the meeting room. Use your five senses. What do you see, smell, hear, and taste? How does your body feel in the chair?

- While driving to or from work, notice how you feel. Where is there tension in your body? Are your shoulders raised? Is your stomach tight? Can you stretch or move your body in a way that dissolves the tension you feel?

- Take a break at work every hour. Take one to two minutes to breathe and become aware of your thoughts, feelings, and body. Connect with yourself in the present moment.

- Engage in formal guided meditation, of which there are many types. To start out, consider using a meditation app such as Headspace or MyLife, which are both available on smartphones as well as via the apps' websites. There are also guided meditations available on YouTube.

Three Strategies for Being Present

Remember, being in the present moment more often is all about awareness first, choice second. Your success is determined by your ability to stay in the present moment. To stay focused on the here and now, commit to staying aware of your focus, moment by moment. You could use these strategies to help you get there.

1. Focus on your breath – If you are alive, you are breathing! Therefore, you can always rely on your breath to guide you back to the present moment. When you notice your mind focusing on the future or the past, gently bring it back to the present using your breath. Take a slow, deep breath, focusing on the movement of the air and your body, and repeat until you feel more present and calm. You could also take a Power Breath (covered in chapter 4): Breathe in slowly through your nose for six seconds, hold the breath for two seconds, and then breathe out slowly through your mouth for seven seconds. Take additional Power Breaths as needed until you feel calm and collected.

2. Use a cue word or phrase to own the moment – To gently direct your mind back to the here and now, try using a cue word such as "focus" or a cue phrase such as "be here now" or "be where your feet are." You could also ask yourself "What's important now?" (WIN) and direct your attention to what's important at the present moment. A few years ago, I was working with an NFL player who was having issues with moving on from the past play and focusing in the huddle. He used "be here now," and it made all the difference.

3. Reframe the pressure as an opportunity – We often see pressure as something to avoid, something that we don't want to experience. We can get stuck in future-based thinking, fearing all the things that could go wrong and imagining the worst-case scenario. But the World's Best view pressure differently. They see pressure as a privilege and a challenge. Instead of avoiding pressure, they reframe the situation as a good thing. They know that if they had not accomplished something wonderful in the past, they wouldn't be in their current situation, capable of rising to the occasion. In their book, *Performing Under Pressure: The Science of Doing Your Best When It Matters Most*, Hendrie Weisinger and J. P. Pawliw-Fry explained that high achievers use the natural tools within themselves to perform their best during moments of high pressure. These natural tools include deep breathing, focusing on the process, and reframing the situation—all tools we have discussed so far. "Reframing" means changing your "lens," or how you are viewing a situation. You can see moments of pressure as opportunities—privileges even. Great things can be accomplished under pressure. Pressure happens *for* you, not *to* you.

GET GRITTY

GET PURPOSE

MASTER THOUGHTS

KNOW SELF

DOMINATE CONTROLLABLES

OWN THE MOMENT

CHOOSE EMOTIONS

OWN WHO YOU ARE

LIVE AND LET GO

COURAGE ZONE

My High Performance Game Plan
OWN THE MOMENT

1. I will practice mindfulness daily—as the World's Best do—to regulate my emotions, reduce amygdala hijacking, and improve my performance.

2. I will decide to stay in the present moment by being aware first, then making a choice second.

3. I will remember the nonjudgmental component of mindfulness and take a step back from my own experience to observe my thoughts and emotions.

4. For each goal I set for my business or life, I will outline "the process"—the small things I need to do along the way.

Now, take a moment to record the following on your Grit Board:

- 3–4 process goals you want to focus on to stay gritty

- A few key phrases such as "Awareness first, choice second"; "Be where my feet are"; or "Stay focused on the process."

My High Performance Power Phrase:
I own the moment. I can do and be anything—right here, right now.

7

Choose Empowering Emotions

3:1

The World's Best
thrive because they regularly experience
positive emotions. They know that when people
experience three positive emotions for every one
negative emotion, they flourish.

Chapter 7

Choose Empowering Emotions

---

*"If you cannot control your emotions,
you cannot control your money."*
—WARREN BUFFETT, CEO OF BERKSHIRE HATHAWAY

Jen True started True Real Estate in 2016 with a big, bold vision: to build an agency with a strong brand, where her agents were proud to work. She described starting her own company as a "huge risk." With only $10,000 in the bank to start, she hired five agents and made a splash with her signature orange branding, an uplifting color that represents risk-taking and adventure—the mentality that she adopted. She told me, "[Just a few months in], I only had $700 in my bank account and couldn't make payroll. That's how fast the money went. I had additional expenses I didn't plan for. I didn't want to go to the local bank and get a loan. We just came out strong with our branding and hit it hard. So, I went to the internet and found a loan-shark company and got $25,000 within two days at 67 percent interest. Now that's risk!" She trusted herself, knowing that she had a plan to pay it off, despite what others close to her thought. She paid the loan off in two short months.

She has since grown True Real Estate to over 50 agents, and her vision is to slowly expand to over 150 agents by 2025. She realizes being slow and careful is important to realizing her vision of growth. She looks for agents with a growth mindset who are open-minded and responsible for their own success. As a leader, she works from her strengths, identified by the StrengthsFinder assessment, which are empathy, achievement, adaptability, responsibility, and relator. Her empathy, in particular, has served her well. "I am able to think about my agents first," she said, "and always put myself in their shoes, considering what they want and need."

When I asked Jen what *failure* means to her and how she responds to it, she said, "I don't think you fail. I think you are guided to where you are supposed to be. You learn and you are guided somewhere else." Given the many highs and lows in real estate—including inconsistent income until you are well established—I asked her what advice she would give to fellow entrepreneurs and salespeople. She answered, "Believe so deeply in your vision. You need to keep the belief and faith. Your mentality is key to your success."

Jen believes that as a leader, it is important to encourage your team members to be uncomfortable to help them be their best and realize their own personal visions. "Some people just don't push because they are content with where they are," she told me. As a leader, it is important to keep encouraging others outside their comfort zones so they continue to grow and learn. This could include encouraging them to move to a new role in the company or encouraging them to adapt a bold vision for their work. Jen said that when she encourages her agents, she tells them, "'Someday you will thank me for pushing your outside your comfort zone.' And they do."

Just as Jen True's story conveys, running a business comes with highs and lows. The highs can feel like summiting a mountain peak ("We got this! Business and life are awesome!"), whereas the lows are like valleys of despair ("I'm exhausted! Can I really make this happen?").

GET GRITTY

GET PURPOSE

MASTER THOUGHTS

KNOW SELF

DOMINATE CONTROLLABLES

OWN THE MOMENT

CHOOSE EMOTIONS

OWN WHO YOU ARE

LIVE AND LET GO

COURAGE ZONE

The Life of an Entrepreneur and Business Leader

I have so much energy! Business is awesome! We got this! I am on top of the world!

Oh no!   *I'm exhausted!*   *Here we go again!*

Instead of allowing themselves to feel the highs and lows as a typical entrepreneur, salesperson, or leader would, the World's Best develop the emotional resilience and agility to pivot and adjust, not getting too high or too low.

As leaders, we need to ride the peaks and valleys with ease, choosing more positive, empowering emotions over disempowering emotions. By choosing to feel good more often, we can flatten the peaks and valleys a bit, as the image shows, with the highs not as high and the lows not as low. The World's Best are able to pivot and adjust quickly to ensure the high and low periods won't last as long. Choosing empowering emotions allows us to stay creative and flexible as well as lead in an intentional way.

The Positivity Ratio

Leaders often spend loads of money, energy, and time seeking

GET
GRITTY

GET
PURPOSE

MASTER
THOUGHTS

KNOW
SELF

DOMINATE
CONTROLLABLES

OWN THE
MOMENT

CHOOSE
EMOTIONS

OWN WHO
YOU ARE

LIVE AND
LET GO

COURAGE
ZONE

the secrets of having a high-performing team. But what if at least part of the solution involved choosing empowering emotions and feeling good more often?

For over thirty years, University of North Carolina at Chapel Hill professor Barbara L. Fredrickson has published research on the power of positive emotions. In her book *Positivity: Top-Notch Research Reveals the 3-to-1 Ratio That Will Change Your Life*, she describes a "Positivity Ratio" that leads to each of us thriving or flourishing individually—meaning we feel as if we are living "the good life." Her research suggests that maintaining a ratio of three positive, empowering emotions (e.g., gratitude, hope, confidence, love, fascination) for every one negative, disempowering emotion (e.g., embarrassment, anger, anxiety, dissatisfaction) throughout our day leads to us thriving and feeling alive. No one can experience the world and grow a business without some stress and trauma. And our goal should not be to completely eliminate disempowering emotions.

You might interpret the word *positivity* to be the opposite or absence of negative emotions. But be careful, because that type of binary thinking keeps us trapped. Sometimes positive emotions can inhibit our ability to address adverse situations, conflicts, or stress. And there is a place for negative emotions in our personal lives as well as our businesses: From an evolutionary perspective, negative emotions can help us avoid danger and overwhelming adversity. Furthermore, they can help us stay motivated, focus on innovation following disappointment, and take action to initiate change and growth. Sometimes negative emotions can even be a springboard to developing grit.

What if someone in your family dies? What if your business has to shut down unexpectedly? Or what if your best employee decides to take a position at a different company? In those situations, negative emotions are appropriate and may even be helpful. The key is to not get stuck in those negative or disempowering emotions—to be emotionally agile. When felt consistently, negative emotions stifle creative thinking and innovation.

In general, feeling more positive emotions throughout our day gives us power. As Fredrickson suggested, these positive, empowering emotions help us broaden and build our physical and mental ability. Positive emotions do more than just help us feel good. When we generate positive emotions, we . . .

- Are more likely to be innovative, creative, and productive.

- Directly enhance team performance, attitude, and behavior.

- See improvements in general health and overall longevity.

- Enhance our capacity for resilience and grit.

- Boost our social skills and build more satisfying relationships.

- Increase dopamine levels in our brain, which promotes enhanced cognitive function.

- More effectively cope with and buffer against symptoms of depression.

- Experience greater success at work and are less likely to quit.

- Are able to cope with changes more effectively.

In 2004, Marcial Losada and Emily Heaphy provided more evidence of this 3-to-1 ratio in the workplace in their findings published in the journal *American Behavioral Scientist*: They observed sixty management teams from a large information-processing corporation, then coded thousands of comments that participants made to one another as either positive (e.g., "That's a terrific idea," "I agree with that," etc.) or negative ("Yeah, like that'll work," "No one would do that," etc.). The lowest-performing team's Positivity Ratio was 0.363 to 1—almost three negative comments for every positive one. The medium-performing teams showed an average Positivity Ratio of 1.855 to 1—almost twice as many positive comments than negative ones. And the highest-performing team had a Positivity Ratio of 5.614 to 1—nearly six positive comments for every negative one. The study also showed that the lowest-performing team also showed more selfishness and personal focus. Bottom line: the average employee performs best when they receive roughly five positive comments for every one negative comment.

This Positivity Ratio described above is very similar to the ratio found in John Gottman's research on harmonious and sustainable marriages. He found that the single biggest determinant to a couple's staying married was the ratio of their positive comments to negative comments. The optimal ratio for couples that stayed married was similar to the ratio for the highest-performing teams in a workplace—around five positive comments for every negative comment. Couples who had a ratio of about three positive comments for every four negative comments ended up getting divorced. Eye-opening, huh?

Again, negative emotions can be helpful in small doses. Leaders who are Pollyannaish or who practice fake positivity aren't doing anyone any favors. None of the results above reported zero negative emotions or comments. And negative feedback can even be helpful, pointing out areas with room for improvement. As Fredrickson said, "When considering positive emotions, more is better, up to a point, and when considering negative emotions, less is better, down to a point."

This powerful evidence on the Positivity Ratio shows why leaders should maintain or move closer to the ideal ratio of 3 to 1 for positive comments.

The Power of Positivity

Positivity is linked to increased discovery, learning, and creativity. So why wouldn't we want to maximize that?

- POSITIVITY > negativity = Flourishing performance/health

- NEGATIVITY > positivity = Declining performance/health

You, your team, and your most intimate relationships thrive on positive emotions and positive feedback.
Let's keep the positivity rollin'!

The Power of Emotional Agility

Again, the words *negative* and *positive* do not mean "bad" and "good," respectively. In fact, all emotions are important and can be helpful. In her book *Emotional Agility: Get Unstuck, Embrace Change, and Thrive in Work and Life*, Dr. Susan David describes that one-third of us judge our emotions as good or bad, or push our emotions aside like we don't want to feel them. Feeling our emotions is one step toward having what she calls *emotional agility*, which is your ability to be "flexible with your thoughts and feelings so that you can respond optimally to everyday situations" (notice she uses the word *respond*, not *react*). Emotional agility has been connected to both well-being and success, and it's a skill we can develop. *Emotional rigidity*, on the other hand, is connected to getting "hooked on" or stuck on thoughts, feelings, and behaviors that don't serve us. Emotional rigidity leads to depression and anxiety.

Emotional agility can also help us be grittier, as an emotionally agile person is able to unhook from difficult emotions or thoughts in order to manage difficulties, setbacks, and obstacles better. At the heart of becoming more emotionally agile is seeing all emotions as valuable. Viewing your emotions with curiosity and compassion helps you realize you don't need to act on every thought, emotion, or idea.

As humans, our thinking can be rigid and repetitive. That's why the first step to becoming more emotionally agile is to gently notice (not judge) when we are "hooked" or stuck on a thought or feeling, practicing self-compassion and mindfulness. The second step is to label your emotions and thoughts. To help you get connected, you could ask yourself "What is it that I am feeling right now?" and "What is the purpose of this emotion?" Labeling your emotions helps you see your feelings and thoughts for what they are—just sources of data that help you understand what is important to you.

GET GRITTY

GET PURPOSE

MASTER THOUGHTS

KNOW SELF

DOMINATE CONTROLLABLES

OWN THE MOMENT

CHOOSE EMOTIONS

OWN WHO YOU ARE

LIVE AND LET GO

COURAGE ZONE

Your thoughts and emotions are not facts, but they do tell you about your values and what you care about. When you "step out" and notice how you are feeling as an observer, you can view your emotions from an objective perspective, to help you consider what led to feeling that way. You can then further distance yourself from the emotion by saying things such as "I am noticing that I am feeling sad right now." Make sure to avoid statements such as "I am [emotion]," because we are not our emotions.

As you continue building your business toward your vision, you will experience stress and discomfort—these emotions help you grow. The key is to avoid statements such as "I am stressed" and instead remind yourself "I am feeling stressed right now because I have an important deadline approaching," for example. Again, you are not your feelings.

The third step to becoming more emotionally agile, according to Dr. Susan David, is to "see [your] emotions as data, not directives," which means the emotions are just information, not calls to action. How we feel does not need to impact what we do or how we act. In fact, we can act independently of how we feel. As Dr. David said, "All emotions have a place, but they are not how you need to act." For example, just because you are going through something tough at home or at work doesn't mean you are a bad person or that you should quit or sell your business, just as receiving negative feedback from an employee doesn't mean you are a bad leader. Those events and the emotions you feel as a result are merely data that informs how you move forward.

You can act independently of how you feel.

The last step to becoming more emotionally agile is to act according to your values—how you want to show up as a leader, salesperson, or entrepreneur every day. What principles do you want to live by? What matters to you? Your values make up your way of being or believing. Values are not goals; instead, they guide you in your actions. Values allow you to get closer to the way you want to live. Identifying your values helps you live in alignment with your true self and future self. Living your values is about letting them guide your intentions, words, actions, and thoughts.

Only you can choose your values. To figure out what they are, ask yourself, "What is important to me in this stage of my life?" Or you could consider what you wrote during the Best Possible Self exercise in chapter 1, further asking yourself, "What values can I adopt today that will be important to my future self?" Our values are like a compass, providing direction so that we can keep moving toward our desired destination. Our values inform our actions—both consciously and subconsciously. As leaders, we need to do more than just say our values—we must practice them. That is why it is so important to consciously choose your values.

Also, our values don't shift by context; we only have one set guiding us. Knowing and consciously choosing your values prevents burnout, helps inform your decision-making process, and assists you when you need to pivot and adjust your business. When we work from and live our core values, we are more likely to experience flow and peak performance. If we are not living our values, we can experience cognitive dissonance, where our actions are incongruent with our beliefs.

There are no "right" or "wrong" values—it is all about what is important to you. Identifying your values requires reflection and deeply personal work, but you and your team are worth the work! You can download a Grit Values Exercise at

GET GRITTY

GET PURPOSE

MASTER THOUGHTS

KNOW SELF

DOMINATE CONTROLLABLES

OWN THE MOMENT

CHOOSE EMOTIONS

OWN WHO YOU ARE

LIVE AND LET GO

COURAGE ZONE

beyondgrit.com/bonus to gain clarity on your values. Dr. Susan David suggests that we each have over one hundred choice points each day, where we can act toward or away from our values. Wow, that's a lot! Clarifying your values can help you make effective decisions as a leader as well as be more emotionally agile, to overcome setbacks and adversity. Consider the purposeful actions you want to take today based on your values.

The Power of Optimism

Several years ago, I was attending a Tony Robbins event in Las Vegas. I had recently finished the Boston Marathon and was proudly wearing my marathon jacket. I spotted a similar jacket in the row in front of me, and during a break, I introduced myself. Mike and I hit it off! After the event, he asked me to lead a workshop on mindset at his construction company in upstate New York, which I agreed to.

The night before the workshop, he and I had dinner, during which he told me that a former employee had recently stolen $270,000 from their company. It surprised me that he said it with little emotion, almost factually. "A quarter of a million dollars?" I said in disbelief.

Instead of having a negative emotional reaction, Mike instead responded with hope, optimism, and a relentless belief that his business would be better because of the misfortune. "My mindset was peace," he said. "I knew we could get through this together." They were able to continue building their business despite the adversity, going on to generate $15 million in sales that year, an increase from $10 million the year before. He said, "The employee stealing our money was the best thing that ever happened to us. Challenges make you so much better for the next thing." Because of the way he optimistically responded as a leader, he and his staff were able to continue building the company, positively impacting tens of thousands of people each year with their work.

Mike's story is a great example of practicing optimism, something that research clearly shows helps build businesses. When you are optimistic, you have a general expectation that good things will happen, the future is bright, and success will continue. You also believe that bad events and setbacks are rare and will not continue. Optimism is a core pillar in building your grit. Two researchers, Frederick Crane and Erinn Crane, summarized twenty-five years of research and literature and found that optimism is correlated with entrepreneurial success and comprises a "defining characteristic of entrepreneurs." The good news? Optimism can be taught. You can train yourself to see difficulties, obstacles, and setbacks as opportunities. And when you do, you maintain your optimism, confidence, and grit. Obstacles and setbacks are a given—it's how you respond to them as a leader that matters the most.

The reason we want to continue cultivating optimism as leaders is because it feels good, plus there are incredible benefits. One longitudinal study, for example, suggests that entrepreneurs' optimism was associated with a great increase in their companies' profits a year later. And as covered in chapter 3, Martin Seligman's research suggests that those who practice optimism live longer lives, perform better and more consistently, make more money, are more loyal, experience less pressure and stress, and have more confidence and resilience. Top entrepreneurs, salespeople, and business leaders see opportunities for success where others do not, even in failure. For example, top entrepreneurs have said the following about the power of optimism:

- Debbi Fields, founder of Mrs. Fields, which is best known for their cookies, suggested that entrepreneurs must be optimistic and able to persevere through failure. An optimist, she said, views failures as leading you in a new and better direction.

- Dave Thomas, founder of Wendy's, said you need a certain "personality to be successful in business," which includes confidence, creativity, goal-orientation, and optimism.

- Lillian Vernon, founder of the Lillian Vernon Corporation, tells prospective entrepreneurs in speeches around the country that entrepreneurship is not a field you should enter if you are not an optimist by your nature.

- Earl Graves Sr., founder of *Black Enterprise* magazine, suggested that successful entrepreneurs are active problem solvers, high-energy, courageous, and optimistic.

- And Stephen M. R. Covey, CEO of the Covey Leadership Center and author of *The Speed of Trust*, said that successful entrepreneurs are optimistic and have a positive-abundance mentality. They believe they will experience future rewards and that abundance is all around them.

How do we continue cultivating optimism? The Three OPP Strategy helps you look at the glass as half-full, not half-empty, and continue to see the opportunities in the difficulties, setbacks, and adversity. The Three OPP Strategy includes two steps:

1. Think of a difficulty you are experiencing right now.

2. Ask yourself, *What are the opportunities here?* Consider *at least three* opportunities that can come from the difficulty. Naming three opportunities pushes you to be creative. If you are anything like my clients, the third opportunity you come up with will probably energize you the most, something you want to focus on going forward. The third idea is often a fresh idea you had not yet considered.

For example, at the beginning of the COVID-19 pandemic, several of my clients were struggling with the transition to working from home, for both themselves and their employees. Here is how one of my clients, Tom, applied the Three OPP Strategy.

1. The difficulty: The COVID-19 pandemic, an uncontrollable factor that impacted everyone around the world, suddenly shut down my office. I feel stressed, overwhelmed, and unsure what to do.

2. The opportunities: (1) It's an opportunity for me to intentionally lead and manage the emotions of my team. (2) It's an opportunity for me to learn about new technology, including apps or programs we can use when we are not in the office and working remotely. (3) It's an opportunity for me to support my team in this transition by providing understanding and caring.

When Tom took a step back and focused on the opportunities, he felt more confident about handling the sudden changes in the world as well as more focused on serving his team, and he felt less self-pity. It also allowed him to consider the new technologies he needed to explore and how he could intentionally lead his team. He told me the Three OPP Strategy allowed him to get "unstuck" and be more emotionally agile.

GET GRITTY

GET PURPOSE

MASTER THOUGHTS

KNOW SELF

DOMINATE CONTROLLABLES

OWN THE MOMENT

CHOOSE EMOTIONS

OWN WHO YOU ARE

LIVE AND LET GO

COURAGE ZONE

Growing Your Gratitude

Gratitude is yet another empowering emotion that has been linked to success in business, sales, and entrepreneurship. As prominent researcher and author on gratitude Robert A. Emmons states, gratitude is "a felt sense of wonder, thankfulness, and appreciation for life." You can show gratitude by counting your blessings and noticing how fortunate you are, or how much worse your circumstances could be. You can express gratitude by thanking the people in your life (family, friends, peers, employees, etc.) or by privately relishing cherished moments. But at the heart of gratitude is the ability to appreciate your life and work as they exist today, in the present moment.

Gratitude is the perfect antidote to negative emotions because it's impossible to feel gratitude at the same time as fear, anxiety, worry, envy, or anger. Gratitude is an intentional practice that heightens our performance and grit. Intentionally practicing gratitude each day can balance out the negativity biases that our brain employs to protect us. Expressing gratitude reminds you to appreciate the small things people do, which many times go unrecognized, and where your business is today, even though you want it to become more. You can also express gratitude for past difficult moments, obstacles, and setbacks because they led you and your business to the present moment.

People who show consistent gratitude also report experiencing more positive emotions and increased energy levels. Gratitude also allows us as leaders to be more forgiving, empathic, and helpful. And those who show more gratitude are also less likely to be depressed, anxious, lonely, envious, and/or neurotic. In fact, the research by Sonja Lyubomirsky—psychology professor at the University of California, Riverside—shows eight reasons that expressing gratitude can boost your happiness.

Expressing gratitude . . .

1. Allows you to savor your experiences.

2. Increases your sense of self-worth and self-esteem.

3. Helps you cope with stress and trauma.

4. Encourages moral behavior and acts of kindness/caring.

5. Helps you build relationships and nurture new ones.

6. Inhibits comparisons with others.

7. Diminishes negative emotions such as anger, bitterness, and greed.

8. Helps you to adjust rapidly to a new circumstance or event.

By being grateful, we tap into what makes us tick, and this helps drive us to do better. Gratitude allows us to fall in love with our work, and when we do that, we are more likely to experience flow and high performance as well as live according to our ikigai.

Practicing gratitude regularly can have a large impact on your life. One study, for example, found that by acknowledging and writing down three things you were thankful for every night for just two weeks had an impact that lasted six months. Another study on gratitude in business published in the journal *Psychology* found three types of gratitude that are all connected to job satisfaction: dispositional gratitude (a personal trait); state gratitude (how a person receives positives from outside sources); and institutionalized gratitude (embedded within an organization, including the people, policies, and practices). What could you do to infuse gratitude into your business or organization? What could you do daily to keep gratitude top of mind for yourself and your team?

GET GRITTY

GET PURPOSE

MASTER THOUGHTS

KNOW SELF

DOMINATE CONTROLLABLES

OWN THE MOMENT

CHOOSE EMOTIONS

OWN WHO YOU ARE

LIVE AND LET GO

COURAGE ZONE

Strategies to Generate Positive Emotions

When left unchecked, negativity can be detrimental to your performance, your family, and your life. Negativity impacts the culture of your family and team. It impacts every aspect of your life. To maintain or continue working toward an ideal Positivity Ratio, here are a few practical strategies:

1. Train Your Managers/Supervisors – According to Gallop research, about 50 percent of employees report leaving a job "to get away from their manager to improve their overall life," not because of money issues or their job responsibilities. Help make positivity part of your workplace culture by starting at the top. Properly training your leadership team is key to reducing turnover and improving engagement in your business.

2. Make Feedback Specific – Praise and positive comments are best when they are specific, genuine, timely, and relevant. These guidelines also apply when giving constructive feedback. Remember that 3-to-1 ratio of positive to negative comments when you provide feedback.

3. Do What You Love Outside of Work – Ideally, we want to experience positive, empowering emotions several times throughout our day. What activities do you currently enjoy outside of work? Maybe you enjoy going out to eat, traveling to new places, spending time with friends, having lunch or coffee with peers, reading, exercising, making music, or being in nature. What activities do you want to spend time doing outside of work regularly to generate more positive emotions? Who would you like to spend more time with to generate more positive emotions? Spending time enjoying the things we love outside of work helps us recover and recharge, which primes us to experience flow the next day at work.

4. Show Your Gratitude – You could show your gratitude in a number of ways:

- Start your day with gratitude as part of the GRIT Morning Routine, outlined in the introduction of this book.

- Write a note, send an email, or visit someone to let them know you appreciate them or what they did for you.

- Set aside time at the start or end of your day to write three things you are grateful for—small things, big things, difficult moments, or the moments you care to celebrate.

- Use grateful words such as *blessed*, *blessings*, *fortunate*, *lucky*, *abundance*, *privileged*, *gifts*, or *givers*—instead of ungrateful words such as *unfortunate*, *unlucky*, *regret*, *disastrous*, *doomed*, *hopeless*, *lack*, or *scarcity*.

Your emotional state is an important factor in building your business to your big, bold vision, as it directs your attention, decision-making, relationships, and, ultimately, your health. When you fuel yourself with empowering emotions, your life, performance, and business will change. Feel empowering emotions like the World's Best!

GET
GRITTY

GET
PURPOSE

MASTER
THOUGHTS

KNOW
SELF

DOMINATE
CONTROLLABLES

OWN THE
MOMENT

CHOOSE
EMOTIONS

OWN WHO
YOU ARE

LIVE AND
LET GO

COURAGE
ZONE

My High Performance Game Plan
CHOOSE EMPOWERING EMOTIONS

1. I commit to striving for a daily Positivity Ratio of at least 3 to 1 for positive, empowering emotions and at least 5 to 1 for positive comments, to help me and my business thrive.

2. I will continue to work on my emotional agility by noticing when I get hooked, then labeling my emotions, accepting how I feel, and connecting with my values.

3. I will choose an optimistic perspective when faced with a difficulty, challenge, or setback, then come up with three opportunities it presents.

4. I will consider the additional list of strategies to generate empowering emotions and try one strategy tomorrow.

Now, take a moment to record the following on your Grit Board:

- Three empowering emotions you want to consistently feel

- A few key phrases such as "3 to 1," "Be an optimist," or "Daily gratitude."

My High Performance Power Phrase:
I choose positivity. I choose to bring an optimistic perspective each day, looking for the opportunity.

8

Own Who You Are

The World's Best

make the conscious choice to show up as themselves every day and in every interaction. They know who they are and own who they are.

Chapter 8

Own Who You Are

"Authenticity is the daily practice of letting go of who we think we're supposed to be and embracing who we are."

—BRENÉ BROWN, RESEARCHER AND AUTHOR

Sarah Richards is one of few woman CEOs in the manufacturing industry. She grew up playing and loving sports, and given it was before Title IX—a law that led to more girls playing organized sports—she found herself playing with the boys. From an early age, she dreamed of being the first girl player on the Minnesota Vikings. "My involvement in sports was very important for me in terms of developing what I needed to be as a woman leader in this industry," she told me. Her time playing sports—which includes over twenty-five years as a PGA golf professional—taught her emotional control, how to have empathy for others, and the importance of striving to win. In 2011, she came to lead Jones Metal as a third-generation owner along with her brother and sister.

She shared with me that she owes much of her authentic leadership style to her athleticism and involvement in sports, where she learned about being herself. She said, "Being an authentic leader means to me that you are yourself in business and in your personal life. You are consistent in both areas and let others see your personality. You're the same person twenty-four hours a day. You also hold yourself to the same expectations that you have for others. Authentic leadership means that you have humility and you are approachable."

Sarah also described that a large part of being an authentic leader is vulnerability. When I interviewed her for this book, she said, "I don't think people trust you as a leader if you don't have some vulnerability. You want to show the real you, tell a joke if that is you. It's important that your people see that you, too, have fears and emotions."

When Sarah returned to her hometown to join the family business as a third-generation owner, she aspired to promote her grandparents' legacy of entrepreneurship and her great-grandmother's legacy of leading as a woman in the community. Since being named as CEO and president, she and her coworkers have spent millions on modernizing technology, transitioning the company to paperless, and streamlining their processes, continuing to make a name in the industry, to the point that other companies come to Jones Metal to tour the facilities and learn about their operation.

The Power of Authentic Leadership

In the past decade, more researchers have studied the power of authentic leadership, which is the process of being your true self as a leader. As Bill George, author of *Discover Your True North: Becoming an Authentic Leader*, said, authenticity is "the gold standard of leadership." In fact, authenticity is a practice; it's not something we have or don't have, but a conscious choice of how we want to live. We can practice authenticity; we can choose to make a decision to be us and be real, instead of trying to be someone we are not.

The effective leaders of today have several traits in common, including authenticity, being purpose-driven, high emotional intelligence, and the ability to learn about themselves from

GET GRITTY

GET PURPOSE

MASTER THOUGHTS

KNOW SELF

DOMINATE CONTROLLABLES

OWN THE MOMENT

CHOOSE EMOTIONS

OWN WHO YOU ARE

LIVE AND LET GO

COURAGE ZONE

"crucible" moments (i.e., the great adversities in life). Whereas ineffective leaders focus more on appearances and being liked, acting in their own self-interest—the type of leaders others report not wanting to follow.

Why should we want to strive to be an authentic leader? Authentic leadership has been connected to increased job performance, trust, and creativity. Most importantly, the act of being who you really are is freeing—you don't need to hide yourself, try to be like anyone else, or compare yourself to others. People want to follow authentic leaders, and we remember them. Authentic leaders know themselves— they understand who they are and are connected with their actions and thoughts. They are also aware of their own values, strengths, perspective, and moral compass.

Many of the topics discussed in this book so far have been connected to authenticity and authentic leadership, so you've already been doing some of the hard work that showing up as an authentic leader takes. In his book *Authentic Leadership: Rediscovering the Secrets of Creating Lasting Value*, Bill George suggests that authentic leaders possess five key attributes—purpose, meaning, values, relationships, and self-discipline—all of which we have discussed in various chapters in this book.

The good news? Authentic leadership can be developed. You are not born with the characteristics of an authentic leader. And you don't need to be at the top of your organization or business to lead or be an authentic leader—you can lead at any point in your career and life. As Brené Brown described in her book *The Gifts of Imperfection*, we can consciously practice authenticity daily. She went on to say that we let go of who we think we should be in order to embrace who we really are—even though we are not perfect. When we mindfully practice authenticity, we are less likely to experience anxiety, blame, resentment, and depression—emotions that can undermine our performance.

When you are an authentic leader, you allow your clients and employees to be themselves. Being yourself as a leader is also connected to your confidence. Leaders who have stable self-esteem, or believe in their value or worth, remain open and are less likely to get defensive when faced with negative feedback. Whereas leaders who act unauthentically may prioritize protecting their ego, lie to others to boost their own image, and get defensive when given negative feedback—all of which prevents them from growing and developing personally and in their leadership. Authenticity is the foundation of performance. To be successful in business and life, you must be yourself. That's how others connect with you. People can tell when you're being phony, and it's a roadblock to connection.

As you think about how you can develop your authentic leadership, consider what it would look like for you to show up 100 percent authentically, guaranteed. What would it take? When you show up 100 percent authentically, you accept who you are, letting go of judgment and the belief that you are not enough. Here are some suggestions based on the research and science of authentic leadership to help you show up 100 percent authentically, guaranteed:

- **Be self-aware** – Understanding yourself and your impact on others is a lifelong journey; therefore, self-awareness should be a daily focus.

- **Be transparent** – Openly share information, and express your true thoughts and feelings in a respectful way.

- **Demonstrate consistency between your values and actions** – Identify and write out your values (the My Values Exercise is available at beyondgrit.com/bonus),

GET GRITTY

GET PURPOSE

MASTER THOUGHTS

KNOW SELF

DOMINATE CONTROLLABLES

OWN THE MOMENT

CHOOSE EMOTIONS

OWN WHO YOU ARE

LIVE AND LET GO

COURAGE ZONE

and consider how your actions can be more aligned with your values.

- **Be balanced in your processing** – Analyze all relevant data in an objective way. Practice seeing the bigger picture, and remember to see problems as puzzles to be solved.

- **Be honest and sincere with others** – Be willing to tell others the hard truth when you need to (even if you don't want to).

- **Be honest with yourself, and admit mistakes when you make them** – This shows vulnerability, which helps you connect with others. Remember that no one is perfect.

When we mindfully and purposefully practice authenticity, we invite peace, gratitude, and happiness into our lives, and this impacts our performance. To be successful in business, you must be yourself.

Owning Your Story

Owning and understanding your story is a critical step in your journey to gaining self-awareness and becoming an authentic leader. As you focus on moving your business to the next level, taking time to understand yourself and explore your story can often get pushed aside. Sometimes leaders hesitate to reflect on their story in fear of it being uncomfortable—they would rather keep it in the past and forget about it. But by examining your story, you open up the opportunity to connect with others and learn more about yourself.

What do I mean by "story"? I'm not offering tips on how to tell good stories. Your story is what you tell yourself about yourself. Your understanding of your story creates your reality about your life and your leadership. As performance psychologist Jim Loehr said in his book *The Power of Story*, "Your life is your story. Your story is your life." Your life and leadership are shaped by how you understand your own personal story, which is comprised of many smaller stories and experiences over your lifetime. These experiences include the impact of your parents, teachers, and/or coaches; leadership experiences in youth, college, or early career; and other impactful experiences that have shaped who you are becoming. When you "own your story," you are proud of what you have overcome, who you are, and how you got where you are, embracing the difficulties that shaped you.

Owning your story also means you understand and can make sense of the times you struggled and the difficulties you experienced. Bill George calls these difficulties and struggles "crucibles." They could be the death or illness of a loved one, loss of employment, personal illness, divorce, growing up in poverty, early failure, or feelings of exclusion and discrimination. Sometimes leaders and entrepreneurs avoid reflecting on their past stories because they think it may be too painful or are unsure of the impact. But understanding your struggles and your crucibles helps you relate to others and understand yourself, which is well worth the investment. You and the impact of your leadership are worth the investment!

Authentic leaders learn to understand their crucibles and reframe their difficulties and struggles. In fact, psychologist Abraham Maslow suggested that tragedy and trauma are *the* most important learning experiences that lead to self-actualization, which is the fulfillment of personal potential. If we don't reframe our crucibles, we live with the belief that we are victims, potentially feeling shame, guilt, and powerlessness, which can hold us back from our

GET GRITTY

GET PURPOSE

MASTER THOUGHTS

KNOW SELF

DOMINATE CONTROLLABLES

OWN THE MOMENT

CHOOSE EMOTIONS

OWN WHO YOU ARE

LIVE AND LET GO

COURAGE ZONE

potential. Without understanding our crucibles, we may not understand how our life experiences shape our current work.

When you reframe your stories, you learn more about yourself and how you got where you are today. This makes it easier to challenge your assumptions and find the passion to continue following your goals and dreams and make an impact in this world. It is not the circumstances, experiences, and factors in your life that have shaped you—it is how you describe those experiences and the story you tell yourself about yourself. Remember in chapter 1 where I talked about being meaning-making machines and how we create meaning constantly in our lives? We can reinterpret the stories from our past and decide to embrace a new meaning.

When you reframe your story, you act and think like a creator, taking control of your mindset and leadership, recognizing you are not a victim of your experiences. Your experiences shaped your leadership and your passion as a business leader, entrepreneur, and/or salesperson. Re-examining the difficulties and struggles in your past can enable transformative experiences that clarify your life's calling and purpose, providing new meaning. You can continue evolving your stories, and when you do, you can live and lead with more clarity, passion, and authenticity.

We all experience struggles and difficulties. And many times, we don't take a step back to see the similarities between our stories. When you own and share your story, you inspire others because you connect with them. You seem real and relatable, which can motivate others to share their true selves too. When you own your story, you let people see you and trust you.

THE JOHARI WINDOW

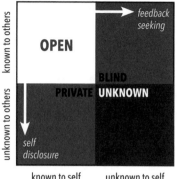
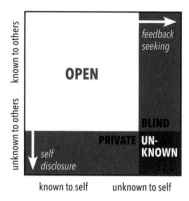

The Johari Window—designed in 1955 by psychologists Joseph Luft and Harrington Ingham—is an exercise that helps us be more open with others and understand how to become more authentic.

Becoming more authentic would mean expanding the top-left quadrant of the window (the section labeled "Open"). On a practical level, that could mean sharing your life story, including your crucibles, with your team and others. It could also mean exposing your weaknesses, admitting your mistakes, and expressing your purpose, values, and motivations. When you share about yourself and your experiences, you open the door (or window) to connect with others.

When I share this concept with my clients, many of them are initially nervous about being more open, vulnerable, and authentic with their employees and clients, fearing it will be met with judgment or rejection. But by sharing more about themselves, they quickly realize it is a way to continue building relationships and connecting with others. Once you take the step to be more vulnerable and share your authentic self with others, you quickly see the impact.

GET GRITTY

GET PURPOSE

MASTER THOUGHTS

KNOW SELF

DOMINATE CONTROLLABLES

OWN THE MOMENT

CHOOSE EMOTIONS

OWN WHO YOU ARE

LIVE AND LET GO

COURAGE ZONE

Notice in the Johari Window that the "Private" section is still present. That's because being authentic doesn't mean you share *all* of your problems, issues, and insecurities with everyone, or even anyone. I really like Brené Brown's description of this idea in her book *Dare to Lead*: she states that vulnerability is needed to build trust and connection and that vulnerability is not the same as disclosure. In her Netflix special, *The Call to Courage*, Brown jokes that live-tweeting your bikini waxing is not vulnerability. Vulnerability is not about the amount of disclosure but the quality and intention behind the disclosure. Brown says that you should "share your story with people who've earned the right to hear your story," and she provides four guiding questions for us to answer before sharing something publicly:

- Why am I sharing this?

- What outcome am I hoping for?

- What emotions am I experiencing?

- What unmet needs might I be trying to meet?

The "Blind" quadrant of the Johari Window represents things that are unknown to you but seen and acknowledged by others. To continue making the "Blind" quadrant smaller, you should continue seeking insights and honest feedback about your blind spots from others you trust. You could ask family or friends directly or even hire a coach like me to help you engage in the process of learning and growing.

Here are a few ways you can continue exploring your authentic self and how that influences your leadership:

- **Consider where you are on your leadership journey** – What action steps would help you lead more authentically?

- **List your core values** – Those are the values that are most important in your life and leadership. (See chapter 7, or visit beyondgritforbuisness.com for an exercise on consciously identifying your values.) Define your values, rank them, and then lead in a way that reflects them.

- **Reflect on and write about your life story** – What peaks and valleys have you experienced that led you to where you are today?

- **Write about how your crucibles have shaped your leadership** – (Again, "crucibles" are your greatest adversities.) How have they shaped your purpose, character, values, leadership, etc.?

- **Analyze an unexplored crucible** – Take one crucible that you have not yet reframed or found the gift or meaning in, and write about your experience or share it with a friend or family member. How did you feel at the time? How did you cope with the experience? How did it shape your worldview, life, and work?

- **Explore the story of your passion** – When you look back at your experiences, what led to identifying your passion?

When you own your story, you begin to connect with it in a deeper way. You are proud of what you have overcome and who you are now. And you inspire others, giving them permission to be an authentic leader too.

Let Go of Internal Barriers

In my work with clients on showing up as an authentic leader and sharing their story to connect with others, they express four main types of barriers, all of which need to be let go—or disempowered, at least—in order to move on:

GET GRITTY

GET PURPOSE

MASTER THOUGHTS

KNOW SELF

DOMINATE CONTROLLABLES

OWN THE MOMENT

CHOOSE EMOTIONS

OWN WHO YOU ARE

LIVE AND LET GO

COURAGE ZONE

1. Judgment

2. Comparison

3. Limiting Beliefs

4. Fear

You may be thinking that letting go of or moving past those barriers is easy—but it's not. The journey involves hard, soul-connecting work and daily mental conditioning. But the good news is, with work, these internal obstacles can be shrunk, and when we shrink them, we are able to live and work more fully. We'll talk about fear extensively in the next practice, about courage. For now, let's dive into how judgment, comparison, and limiting beliefs get in the way of being ourselves, showing up as authentic leaders, and ultimately reaching our potential and becoming a high performer.

Letting Go of Judgment

I recently completed Shirzad Chamine's Positive Intelligence Coach Training to gain more of an understanding of how our "Saboteurs" (internal barriers) get in our way as well as how to channel what he describes as our "Sage perspective" (our true essence). I took the training primarily to provide more value to my own clients, but I also knew I needed to reduce my internal judgment. I'd noticed how my internal judge was getting in the way of my happiness and performance at times, especially over the last year, having received some tough feedback and being reminded I hadn't reached my own goals. I was tired of my judge's impact, and I was ready to make a change! Chamine, a Stanford lecturer and *New York Times* bestselling author of the book *Positive Intelligence*, explains that "Most successful and high-achieving people are tortured by their own judge."

The internal judge is the universal saboteur—we all have one. The judge's universal advantage is that it never goes away, enduring as an automatic mental habit that informs our thinking, feelings, and actions. As Chamine describes, your judge was developed during childhood to keep you safe, but in adulthood, your judge can severely limit your success and happiness. Judgment compels you to find faults in yourself, your circumstances, your family, your business, your team, and all other people. We all judge ourselves and one another, often without recognizing it.

In general, we judge in three ways:

1. We judge ourselves.

2. We judge others.

3. We judge events and circumstances.

When we judge ourselves, we think, *What is wrong with me? What is wrong with you? What is wrong with the things around me?* My own internal judge is ugly and says things like, *No one will read this book anyway, so why write it?; I'd rather just work on my easier to-do items than take a risk by posting on social media, where I may not get as many likes as I want*; and, *No one will listen to me anyway, so why speak up?* When I write these words on paper, I know they are lies. But it's so easy to believe our internal judge, isn't it? Wow, our mind is powerful! But it's freeing to remember that our internal judge is just an automatic mental habit, and the key is to consciously and proactively choose your focus.

Your judge might tell you, *I can't be happy with my current circumstances*, meaning, *I can't be happy with my current business, my current lifestyle, or my family. I need that new business, house, career, relationship, etc.* Your judge generates anxiety, stress, anger, shame, and guilt. When your judge is loud and activated, it prevents you from experiencing flow, creativity, empathy, curiosity, and change.

Our judge holds us back from making the impact we want to make. I recently heard Chamine say, "When you judge

GET GRITTY

GET PURPOSE

MASTER THOUGHTS

KNOW SELF

DOMINATE CONTROLLABLES

OWN THE MOMENT

CHOOSE EMOTIONS

OWN WHO YOU ARE

LIVE AND LET GO

COURAGE ZONE

for more than one second, you are sabotaging yourself." I instantly stopped what I was doing. That day, my mind was blown, and I recommitted to reducing my judge. If you want to reduce your judge, the first step is to witness it without judgment. Each day, you need to acknowledge your judge for what it is, which, over time, will take away its power.

The first step to reducing your judge is noticing it—without judgment.

Next, show yourself some compassion, and soften your internal voice. When I write, my judge is always activated at some point, so before I sit down to write, I tell myself something like, "Hey, Cindra. Remember that this book will make a real difference in people's lives. It's important to keep going." Each time we recognize our judge and soften our internal voice, we establish or strengthen a new neural pathway in our brain, reducing our judge and its power over our feelings, thoughts, and actions.

Letting Go of Comparison

As a business leader, entrepreneur, and/or salesperson, it's easy to get caught up in the competition, comparing yourself to others instead of focusing on the things you control. Unfortunately, we live in a culture of comparison. And when we compare ourselves to others, we rarely do so in a fair way. Insteadm we usually put someone else's highlight reel up against our bloopers or B-roll, or their story's middle or end up against our beginning. I see new entrepreneurs do this all the time. They compare themselves and their lack of success or small early successes to the large, booming businesses that have been thriving for ten, twenty, or even fifty years.

It's natural to wonder how you place or where you fit in the world, but comparing yourself to others can be a trap. Comparison is a ten-foot barrier standing in the way of you showing up as your authentic self, and it leads to a frenzy of self-doubt. When you compare yourself, your business, or your performance to others, you can drain your confidence. Comparison can stop your dreams, passions, and motivations, inhibiting your ability to stay gritty. Researchers have also found that comparison leads to anxiety, depression, loneliness, and chronic insecurity.

When we compare ourselves to others, we have a hard time being happy for other people and their successes. The happiest and most successful people take pleasure in other people's successes. Acknowledge the other person, and be excited for their success. Remember that comparison is an automatic mental habit that you can reduce. Try asking yourself, "What can I learn from this person?" or "How can I see this person as a role model?" And while doing so, avoid any comparison to yourself. Learning from someone you admire is the best way to make massive gains in your performance and your business.

To keep your focus and energy on being the best you, think back to how far you, your performance, and your business have come. Compare where you are today with where you were one, three, or five years ago. And when you notice you're comparing yourself to someone else, acknowledge it without judgment, then turn your attention back to being the best authentic you that you can be. Amazing things can happen when you focus on putting your best foot forward, one client, presentation, or sale at a time.

Letting Go of Limiting Beliefs

Limiting beliefs are yet another mental barrier to becoming an authentic leader or high performer. We all experience limiting beliefs, but if not examined, they can be

GET GRITTY

GET PURPOSE

MASTER THOUGHTS

KNOW SELF

DOMINATE CONTROLLABLES

OWN THE MOMENT

CHOOSE EMOTIONS

OWN WHO YOU ARE

LIVE AND LET GO

COURAGE ZONE

detrimental to your potential as a business leader. Underlining everyone's limiting beliefs is feeling as if you are not enough—not smart enough, not successful enough, not good-looking enough, not tall enough, not talented enough . . . The list goes on and on.

Can you hear the underlying judgment in those statements? In my experience, the limiting belief that most often gets in the way of authentic leadership is the belief that others won't appreciate, like, or respect you if you put forth your true self. When we give into the illusion, or lie, that we are not enough, we're not embracing ourselves, our strengths, or the value we bring to this world. Listening to your judge in such cases stops you in your tracks.

You are enough just the way you are—smart enough, talented enough, and successful enough to build your business to a bold future. We must address our limiting beliefs because they hold us back. When we do this, we let go of our baggage and are free to be our authentic selves. You have the power to address the limiting beliefs that are holding you back!

You are enough just the way you are—smart enough, talented enough, and successful enough to build your business to a bold future.

Limiting beliefs related to money is the barrier I see entrepreneurs, business leaders, and salespeople struggle with the most, and those beliefs greatly restrict their potential. Many people have a complex relationship with money, often stemming from how they were raised and what they were taught. These limiting beliefs about money sound like . . .

- There is never enough money to go around.

- Money is the root of all evil.

- People that are rich are greedy, selfish, snobby, and/or lucky.

- Money doesn't grow on trees.

- No one in our family ever made real money.

- Save your money for a rainy day.

- You have to have money to make money.

- The rich get richer.

To continue building a successful business, you must examine the *external* ways of generating more revenue as well as the *internal* beliefs that drive your decisions around money. These unconscious beliefs that take place outside your conscious awareness impact your behaviors and emotions. For example, several years ago I worked with a financial planner, Ted, as his executive coach. As we began working together, we uncovered the limiting belief that he was from a small town and couldn't be successful. This belief manifested as statements such as "I am from [small town], and no one from there is successful" and "People from where I grew up don't make that kind of money." Together, we worked on identifying this limiting belief and its impact on his life, then replaced the limiting belief with a new, empowering belief: "People from small towns all over the world have been successful, and I can be successful regardless of where I grew up." Replacing his old belief with a new belief didn't happen overnight; it took awareness and a commitment, on Tom's end, to believe a more empowering thought. Many times, the limiting beliefs we hold were reinforced for many years by us and those around us, so it

GET GRITTY

GET PURPOSE

MASTER THOUGHTS

KNOW SELF

DOMINATE CONTROLLABLES

OWN THE MOMENT

CHOOSE EMOTIONS

OWN WHO YOU ARE

LIVE AND LET GO

COURAGE ZONE

takes conscious awareness to believe something different about ourselves, our business, or our potential.

When I began speaking as part of my business, delivering keynotes and corporate trainings, I had to be aware of my limiting beliefs about money (and still do!). My colleagues on the speaking circuit told me I should've been charging thousands and thousands of dollars to deliver a talk. I couldn't believe or imagine that someone would pay me that much to share my perspective. I had to increase my awareness of the liming beliefs I held about my value and impact. Even today, each time I increase my keynote or training fees, I need to upgrade my beliefs about myself and my value just as much. To do that, I start each morning with my GRIT Morning Routine and Priming Exercise (page 15). The following Power Phrases, in particular, are especially important for me to believe because they directly impact the value I bring to the world:

- I know my value and the value of my work to this world.

- I learn as if I change millions of people's lives.

- The tools I teach change people's lives.

And then, throughout my day, I also keep tabs on how my limiting beliefs about money and my value play out.

People frequently ask me, "Cindra, what's the difference between a thought and a belief?" The difference is that you have thousands of thoughts each day—between seventy thousand and ninety thousand, according to the National Science Center. None of your thoughts have power unless you give it to them. A belief is a thought that *you* believe, that *you* make real, and that *you* accept as true. That's powerful and freeing to recognize, because you also have the power to not believe everything you think! Beliefs are created over a long period of time, through a consistent way of thinking.

Beliefs created over a shorter period of time are generally easier to break, whereas beliefs formed over many, many years are more entrenched and take more work to change.

To address your limiting beliefs, follow the four steps described below, and keep in mind that they may seem simple, but they will take effort and conscious awareness:

1. First, ask yourself, "What are my limiting beliefs about myself, what I can do, and the world?" Gently acknowledge your limiting beliefs without judgment. When you notice limiting beliefs popping into your mind and awareness during your day, write them down so you can examine them later. Examples of limiting beliefs that may be holding you back include:

- I am not courageous enough to build my business's revenue up to $ _____.

- I am from _____, and people from there don't succeed.

- No one will ever buy that product from me.

- You can't make money doing _____.

- It's impossible to have a family *and* do the work I love.

- I have to work hard to make money.

2. Without judgment, take a moment to explore that limiting belief. You could ask yourself one or more of these reflective questions to consider how the limiting belief has impacted your work, your life, and your happiness:

- How true is this belief?

- What evidence do I have to support this belief?

- Where did this belief come from?

GET GRITTY

GET PURPOSE

MASTER THOUGHTS

KNOW SELF

DOMINATE CONTROLLABLES

OWN THE MOMENT

CHOOSE EMOTIONS

OWN WHO YOU ARE

LIVE AND LET GO

COURAGE ZONE

- How has this belief affected me?

- How has this belief limited me?

3. Now, let's replace the belief. Ask yourself what belief would allow you to become all you could be? This could be the opposite belief of the limiting belief you acknowledged in step 1. Repeat this step until you have acknowledged all of the limiting beliefs you identified. Example replacement beliefs include . . .

- I will choose courage each day, and I will build my business to $ _____ in revenue.

- People from small towns everywhere can succeed.

- My clients need the products I offer.

When Jack Canfield—the author of all those Chicken Soup for the Soul books as well as my favorite book, *The Success Principles*—and I were talking about limiting beliefs around money on my podcast, *High Performance Mindset*, episode 351, he suggested these *empowering* beliefs about money:

- "Money is the root of all generosity."

- "Money is the root of all generous giving in my family."

- "Money is the root of great education for my children."

Do you see how he reframed the old saying? The same reframing strategy could be applied to other limiting beliefs.

4. Lastly, close your eyes, and imagine your new, empowering belief is true. What would your business and life look like once you start living these new, empowering beliefs each day? Imagine your future in detail. Then start noticing all the ways your new belief is proven true in your life and business.

(I've included a Limiting Beliefs Meditation in the bonus materials at beyondgritforbusiness.com/bonus to help you let go of your limiting beliefs. I think you will like it!)

As a business leader, entrepreneur, and/or salesperson, you can't afford to let limiting beliefs become invisible barriers. When you limit yourself, you allow others to limit you too. When you replace limiting beliefs, doors will open, and you will attract the best that you deserve. You will lead more authentically and purposefully. The world needs you and your gifts. Don't hold back!

GET GRITTY

GET PURPOSE

MASTER THOUGHTS

KNOW SELF

DOMINATE CONTROLLABLES

OWN THE MOMENT

CHOOSE EMOTIONS

OWN WHO YOU ARE

LIVE AND LET GO

COURAGE ZONE

My High Performance Game Plan
OWN WHO YOU ARE

1. I commit to being an authentic leader. I will consider where I am on my journey to authentic leadership as well as the steps I need to take.

2. I'll begin to write my story, identifying and reframing the crucibles in my life and sharing them with others.

3. When I get caught up comparing myself to others, I will instead choose to celebrate their successes by complimenting them or sharing what I've learned from them.

4. I will consider my limiting beliefs that act as invisible barriers to my authentic self and choose new, empowering beliefs to adopt.

Now, take a moment to record the following on your Grit Board:

- Five words that describe you as an authentic leader

- A few key phrases such as "100 percent authentic, guaranteed"; "Own my story"; "Notice my judge without judgment"; or "Defeat my limiting beliefs."

My High Performance Power Phrase:

The world needs me and my gifts. I will show my authentic self to the world through my leadership.

9

Live and Let Go

MISTAKES

The World's Best

know that people are not perfect.
They are kind to themselves, let go of
their mistakes quickly after learning from
them, and decide to live life full-out.

Chapter 9

Live and Let Go

"You have been criticizing yourself for years and it hasn't worked. Try approving of yourself and see what happens."—LOUISE HAY, AUTHOR

J ay Abdo's dad, Joe, was born in Mankato, Minnesota, in 1930 and was the youngest of the thirteen children of his Lebanese immigrant parents. After taking eight years to finish his degree, balancing working as a bookkeeper in a local hardware store and providing for his wife and five children, Joe became the first in the nation to pass his CPA exam before graduating from college. His mother, a widow, loaned him $13,000—basically her life savings—to start his own solo accounting firm. Joe was a hard-working, ethics-driven man.

Jay got involved in the family business at the age of twenty-five to help expand the firm. Today, Abdo has two offices, over 180 employees, and twenty partners. Later, as a family, they started Northland Securities, BankVista, and ABDO (a nationally recognized family of educational publishers). Altogether, their companies now have over five hundred employees.

When I interviewed Jay for this book, I could tell he cared deeply about people, and I asked him how his dad's business practices shaped their family's success and what they have built. Jay shared many practices with me, but balancing risk was a key factor. He said, "My dad took risks and evaluated the risks a lot, considering how much money it would take, how much percentage we should put down, and then acknowledging that we must be ready to perform. So, there was a lot of due diligence in taking risk. We always took a balanced risk when we felt it was the right risk to take." Jay also learned the importance of caring for his people, building relationships, and reinvesting in the company to best serve the clients and employees. "A true entrepreneur is someone that reinvests their profits [in their business]. . . . Your employees need to see that they can grow inside the company."

When I asked Jay to share his success tips for any entrepreneur and business leader, he said the following:

- Hiring good people is an essential part of success. Pay them well, and mentor them, but don't be so demanding that they want to work somewhere else.

- Reinvest constantly, and make sure you have the very best technology for your people.

- Reward your people. The more successful your employees are, the more successful you will be.

- It takes a positive attitude to build a strong business. You can't let rejection get you down.

- Never burn a bridge with an old client. If they leave because of fees, or whatever reason, let them know that your door is always open if they ever change their mind. I've had clients ask me to take them back years later because I kept the door open.

- When providing feedback to your employees, be honest and straightforward, but follow up with them a day or two later to check in. This shows you care about them as a person.

GET GRITTY

GET PURPOSE

MASTER THOUGHTS

KNOW SELF

DOMINATE CONTROLLABLES

OWN THE MOMENT

CHOOSE EMOTIONS

OWN WHO YOU ARE

LIVE AND LET GO

COURAGE ZONE

As I interviewed Jay, I could see how Abdo would be ranked as one of the top places to work in any community. They have one of the lowest employee-turnover percentages in the field because they put people first.

Practicing Self-Compassion

The World's Best—entrepreneurs, salespeople, and leaders—have very high standards and expect success, otherwise they wouldn't be where they are. Yet they also understand the importance of being kind to yourself—they let go of mistakes quickly while protecting their energy, confidence, and momentum.

Self-compassion—the practice of being kind to yourself in times of failure or pain—can run counter to the belief that we should be critical of ourselves to get ahead. We might believe that the harder we are on ourselves, the quicker we'll get to our goal. For many years, I believed that the more critical I was of myself, the better I would perform or the more I would achieve. It's actually quite the opposite! I wish I had learned this lesson earlier—it could have prevented a lot of suffering. And that is why it's so great *you* are hearing this now.

To be our best and build our business to our vision, we need to strive toward self-compassion, as opposed to self-criticism. Many people grow up not being taught that the practice of self-compassion is essential to our success; so it's no surprise that many entrepreneurs, leaders, and salespeople have a hard time being kind to themselves, mostly because they don't realize the importance. Oftentimes, we think that self-compassion could lead to complacency or a lack of motivation, productivity, or achievement. But the opposite is true.

A leading researcher on self-compassion, Dr. Kristin Neff has found an array of positive benefits and rewards to practicing self-compassion, including the following:

- Higher levels happiness, optimism, and positive affect

- Greater emotional resilience and less reactive anger

- More personal initiative, curiosity, and exploration

- Higher agreeableness, extroversion, and conscientiousness

- Less anxiety, depression, rumination, and thought suppression

- Higher life satisfaction and emotional intelligence

- More caring relationship behavior and social connectedness

- Increased likelihood of reaching mastery goals and less fear of failure

That last one—that self-compassion is positively related to achieving mastery goals—suggests that those who are more compassionate with themselves are better able to stay motivated and see failure as an opportunity at the same time. And by not harshly judging yourself or blowing your failures out of proportion, you are better able to stay confident in your ability to learn.

University of California, Berkeley's Juliana Breines and Serena Chen asked a powerful question in their research study on self-compassion: could treating oneself with compassion after making a mistake increase motivation? After conducting four separate studies, they concluded, "These findings suggest that, somewhat paradoxically, taking an accepting approach to personal failure may make people more motivated to improve themselves." They explained, for example, that those who showed self-compassion had greater motivation to change a weakness and spent more time studying for a difficult test after failure.

GET GRITTY

GET PURPOSE

MASTER THOUGHTS

KNOW SELF

DOMINATE CONTROLLABLES

OWN THE MOMENT

CHOOSE EMOTIONS

OWN WHO YOU ARE

LIVE AND LET GO

COURAGE ZONE

When I teach my executive clients about self-compassion and they practice it, they tell me that they perform better, that they are happier, less stressed, and kinder to others at work, and that they are kinder with their families. When we discuss self-compassion in our coaching sessions, we talk about not avoiding or denying our suffering, because it is part of the human experience. All people suffer—that is part of being human—and we are all imperfect. When we practice self-compassion, we show ourselves the same kindness we would show others when they fail. Who ever said we should be perfect, anyway? Likely no one!

When we practice self-compassion, we remind ourselves that all humans experience feelings of suffering, inadequacy, and not being enough. We realize we are not alone, that all humans go through difficulties, so there is no need to feel self-pity. My executive coaching sessions also incorporate talking about how to gain the tools, skills, and wisdom to reduce suffering. Getting stuck in suffering doesn't help.

In her book *Self-Compassion: The Proven Power of Being Kind to Yourself*, Dr. Neff provides three elements of self-compassion:

- **Self-kindness vs. self-judgment** – Being warm and kind to ourselves when we fail, make a mistake, or feel inadequate, rather than ignoring our pain or judging or criticizing ourselves. Being self-compassionate means we recognize that experiencing difficulties, failing, and being imperfect is inevitable because we are human.

- **Common humanity vs. isolation** – Acknowledging that suffering and feelings of personal inadequacy are part of the shared human experience, rather than something that happens to you alone.

- **Mindfulness vs. overidentification with thoughts** – Taking a balanced, nonjudgmental approach to observing our negative emotions so we don't suppress or exaggerate our feelings. We can observe our negative thoughts and emotions with openness and avoid overidentifying by observing—not suppressing or denying—how we feel. Remember, you don't need to believe everything you think!

Staying gritty and reaching high performance requires adopting the mindset of constant and never-ending improvement. To reach your goals and to stay current and relevant, you need to constantly evolve your skills and mindset. Showing self-compassion is key to adapting to the ever-changing marketplace and bouncing back quickly after setbacks, adversity, and mistakes. Self-compassion is also a powerful antidote to stress, anxiety, and perfectionistic thinking, which can lead to poor performance. When we practice self-compassion, we reduce our tendency to ruminate on our problems or negative thoughts. We can avoid the traps of listening to our critical inner voice and developing limiting beliefs.

Showing compassion with others is similar to showing yourself compassion. I have found—and this is true of my clients as well—that the more compassionate I am with myself, the more compassionate I can be with others. Showing compassion is an essential skill for leaders and managers. It starts with noticing how the other person is feeling, then showing them empathy with warmth, care, and a desire to help. Remember to offer understanding and kindness when they make mistakes or fail, instead of judging them harshly. They are likely already judging themselves harshly, so there's no reason to add to that. By offering empathy and understanding, you help build a team and culture of trust, demonstrating that those you lead don't need to be perfect.

GET GRITTY

GET PURPOSE

MASTER THOUGHTS

KNOW SELF

DOMINATE CONTROLLABLES

OWN THE MOMENT

CHOOSE EMOTIONS

OWN WHO YOU ARE

LIVE AND LET GO

COURAGE ZONE

Embracing Mistakes = Psychological Safety

Google, which is used for 70 percent of online searches worldwide, is at the heart of many of our experiences on the internet. (It's my search engine of choice—how about you?) In 2012, Google undertook a massive two-year study on high-performing teams, calling it "Project Aristotle." They sought to answer the question *What makes a high performing team?* After conducting over 200 interviews and looking at over 250 attributes of 180 Google teams, they surprisingly found a top ingredient for high-performing teams was psychological safety—in fact, it was the *most* important ingredient in high-performing teams and actually underpinned the other ingredients.

Psychological safety is a person's belief that they can take risks without feeling insecure, embarrassed, or as if they will be punished. Employees who experience psychological safety feel comfortable trying new things, asking questions, and admitting mistakes—all of which lead to creativity and innovation. Those that experience psychological safety are free to take interpersonal risks, confident that neither they nor any other members of their team will be rejected, punished, or embarrassed when speaking up. At the heart of psychological safety is mutual respect and trust, regardless of where you are on the organizational chart.

Dr. Amy Edmondson, a professor and researcher at the Harvard Business School, coined the term *psychological safety*, which she defines as "a shared belief held by members of a team that the team is safe from interpersonal risk-tasking." When studying high-performing teams, she expected that they would make fewer mistakes than lower-performing teams. What she found was the opposite—high-performing teams actually made *more* mistakes! The biggest factor that impacted the difference in performance between the lower-performing and high-performing teams was the *way* they approached their mistakes. Instead of hiding their mistakes, the high performers admitted their mistakes and shared them as opportunities for others to learn and their organization to grow. The members of the high-performing teams created an environment where it was okay, or "safe," to fail. Members of those teams felt accepted and respected.

Creating psychological safety leads to more innovation and higher performance.

Studies have shown that psychological safety allows for creativity, moderate risk taking, and speaking your mind—all of which can help you and your business make breakthroughs and achieve higher performance. Project Aristotle also found that individuals on teams with higher psychological safety were less likely to leave Google and were "more likely to harness the power of good ideas from their teammates." The high performers that felt greater psychological safety brought in more revenue and were rated twice as effective by executives.

Psychological safety can also help prevent an amygdala hijack, something we discussed in chapter 4. When under stress, your amygdala disables your frontal lobe, where your rational thinking takes place, and activates your fight-or-flight response. When you create psychological safety on your team and within your business, your people are more likely to use the front, rational part of their brain, leading to more creativity, greater focus, and stronger pursuit of internal goals.

A recent Gallup poll showed that only three out of every ten people feel their opinion matters at work—only 30 percent! You can change that statistic in your own business by deciding to create more psychological safety. When you create a culture of psychological safety, people feel comfortable expressing their opinions because they know their opinions matter. Your

GET GRITTY

GET PURPOSE

MASTER THOUGHTS

KNOW SELF

DOMINATE CONTROLLABLES

OWN THE MOMENT

CHOOSE EMOTIONS

OWN WHO YOU ARE

LIVE AND LET GO

COURAGE ZONE

people will be less likely to leave and more likely to tap into their creativity and innovation. As a result, your business will be more likely to reach your bold vision. And when people feel like their voice makes a difference, there is less turnover and more productivity. For example, one group of researchers found that when at least six out of every ten employees feel like their opinion matters, there is 27 percent less turnover and 12 percent more productivity as a result.

One of my favorite stories of a leader creating psychological safety is IBM's former CEO Tom Watson Jr. He once said, "The fastest way to succeed is to double your failure rate." And when his employees failed, he didn't punish them; instead, he let this idea guide his actions. He believed that when working on complex systems, success is rarer than failure, and there is always an opportunity to learn and grow when outcomes are not met.

One day he called his vice president into his office because his failed developmental project had cost IBM $10 million. When the vice president came in the room, he said to Tom, "I expect you're wanting me to submit my resignation now." Tom responded, "God, no, we just spent several million dollars educating you on what does and what doesn't work. We want you to be here." What I love about Tom's response is that he adopted the perspective that failure is what we do, not who we are. When we believe *we* are the failure, we feel inadequate, and our confidence suffers. Tom also reminded his vice president of his value to the company, something many of us tend to forget, especially after a failure.

Everyone fails. The people and teams who fail the most and the fastest succeed.

GET
GRITTY

GET
PURPOSE

MASTER
THOUGHTS

KNOW
SELF

DOMINATE
CONTROLLABLES

OWN THE
MOMENT

CHOOSE
EMOTIONS

OWN WHO
YOU ARE

LIVE AND
LET GO

COURAGE
ZONE

High-performing teams embrace the value of "failing fast" and realize that fear is not an effective motivator. They know that the word *failure* can be misleading. Mistakes are not failures as long as you and your team embrace them openly, measure them, and respond to new information and learning in a positive and constructive way. One of the teams I work with even *rewards* failure—they give a trophy to the person or the team that made "the biggest mistakes" in a time period on a particular project. The goal is to "fail faster." When we celebrate people learning and growing, our teams feel safer, we create a positive culture, and innovation is more likely to happen.

Here are a few ways to improve the psychological safety within your business and on your team:

- If you don't feel your business culture supports this idea of "failing faster," start a conversation about how to change it.

- Use Amy Edmondson's measure of psychological safety by asking your team to indicate how strongly they agree or disagree with statements such as "It is safe to take a risk on this team."

- Remember that psychological safety is not just about being nice or lowering performance standards.

- Encourage your team to talk openly about mistakes, errors, and failures transparently, remembering we learn best from failure.

- Encourage your team to have regular conversations about what went right, what went wrong, what can be changed, and what will keep things moving forward.

- Acknowledge your own mistakes and how you, too, can be wrong. Show yourself the same compassion you would for others.

- Model curiosity and ask questions with the intention of learning from everyone in your business, regardless of where they are in the organization chart.

- Share with your team the message that failure is acceptable, then make sure you don't only reward those who succeed.

- Be open to the voices of everyone in your business, and acknowledge when team members contributed to a success or a decision.

- When members of your team fail, remember to listen, offer help, and look forward by discussing what they learned and what you can learn. Then brainstorm ways to move forward.

Consider what you could do to increase the psychological safety within your team. Perhaps choose two or three of the ideas above to implement. What if you started creating more psychological safety today? What impact would that have on your business? How would it help you reach your Limitless Vision?

What Is Failure to You?

I've had the privilege of interviewing hundreds of experts on mindset and grit on the *High Performance Mindset* podcast, which we've produced since 2015. During nearly every interview, I ask the guest to describe what failure means to them and then share a time they failed, so we can learn from their failure. It's one of my favorite questions to ask. Below are a few definitions of *failure* that experts have shared; as you are reading, consider how *you* define it.

Jack Canfield is the bestselling author of the Chicken Soup for the Soul series. He submitted the first book to 142 publishers and was rejected. He said, "Failure is simply a delay in results. You're working toward something, and you tried something, and it didn't work. We learn to walk by falling down. If our parents had said 'If you fall down twenty more times, you are just a serial failure, and we're not going to work with you anymore,' no one would ever do that. F-A-I-L—if you take *I* and put a little line on it, it becomes F-A-L-L. When we fall down, we get up" (episode 351).

Anne Grady—keynote speaker, trainer, and author on resilience—said, "I love the acronym for FAIL—First Attempt in Learning. No great success story ever came without significant failure, including people like Oprah, J. K. Rowling, Steven Spielberg, Dr. Seuss, and Colonel Sanders. There's just no example of amazing achievement without a ton of failure. Failure is necessary. So now I see it as a skill-building exercise and ask myself *What can I try next so that I learn from it?*" (episode 353).

Dr. Michael Gervais—creator of the *Finding Mastery* podcast and sport psychologist to the Seattle Seahawks—said, "Failure is part of life, and taking swings at things is part of it. Keep swinging at what you want. I also see failure as when I know I have something to say or to do and I hold back. Failure is any time I am not being authentic" (episode 323).

Zach Brandon—mental-skills coordinator for the Arizona Diamondbacks—said, "The challenge with failure is that we experience this visceral reaction to it. Since childhood, we've been told that failure is this bad thing—it's this thing we should avoid, and we've developed a fear or an aversion toward it, which carries on into adulthood. The perspective is really important in how you view failure as an opportunity to learn. Do you treat a failed event as a devastation, or an education? And how do you learn from the failure?" (episode 349).

Jim Afremow—mental-skills coach and author of *The Champion's Mind*—said, "I look at failure as just not showing up. Woody Allen said that 80 percent of success is just showing up. Let's say I want to run a marathon—I go for it and show up. For me, it was *I don't know how to write a book—I'm going to write one anyway*" (episode 345).

Carey Lohrenz—author, keynote speaker, and the first female F-14 Tomcat pilot in the US—said, "Everybody experiences failure very differently. What I might perceive as failure may be very different from what someone else does. The thing that I find the most damaging on a personal level is the failure to try. That is the thing that leaves me saddled with guilt, with resentment, with negative self-talk, that I can look back and go *I cannot believe I didn't go for it*" (episode 339).

Amy Morin—TEDx speaker and bestselling author of *13 Things Mentally Strong People Don't Do*—said "Failure is proof that I tried hard, that I put myself out there and tried to do something that was outside my comfort zone" (episode 331).

Alan Stein Jr.—performance coach and author of *Raise Your Game*—said, "I'm a firm believer that as long as you give your best effort, you're preparing, and you have a good attitude, you should be pushing yourself to failure in almost every area of your life. Failure is really just the conduit to growing and improving. If you're willing to have the humility and vulnerability to examine a failure after you've experienced it, there's always going to be a lesson or an opportunity. You can grow and develop to be better than you were before" (episode 329).

Mistakes and failure are inevitable, and they're essential in order for us to perform at our very best. To be at our best, we must embrace failure. We often think of failure as any time we don't meet our own expectations or reach our goals. Or maybe you would consider failure to be similar to Michael Gervais's definition—anytime you are not being authentic or are holding back. Consider your answer to these very important questions about failure:

1. What is the definition of failure that you want to guide your life and business?

2. How has failure gotten you to where you are today?

3. How could you help your team learn from and embrace failure?

When you define failure on your terms, the way it serves you, it takes out the sting, and you are able to see the failure as objective and not take it personally. You are not the failure—the failure is an event! When you look back at your past failures and see that they have served a purpose, perhaps they are *the reason* you are where you are today. Perhaps your failures are included in your crucible moments—your greatest adversities in your life. How have your failures been a gift and opportunity?

As you consider how you want to define failure, remember not to see yourself as a failure. When we do that, we can become hopeless. Some people internalize failure and see it as a reflection of themselves, as validation of their negative self-talk. But you are not your mistakes! Remember, failure is an event, not a person. Zig Ziglar said it best: "Failure is an event, never a person; an attitude, not an outcome; a temporary inconvenience; a stepping stone. Our response to it determines just how helpful it can be."

GET GRITTY

GET PURPOSE

MASTER THOUGHTS

KNOW SELF

DOMINATE CONTROLLABLES

OWN THE MOMENT

CHOOSE EMOTIONS

OWN WHO YOU ARE

LIVE AND LET GO

COURAGE ZONE

Learn, Burn, & Return

If you don't practice self-compassion daily and move on from mistakes or failures, you risk burning out, feeling rejected, or giving up on your business. It's easy to beat yourself up, take mistakes personally, and believe it's all about you. But *you* know it's essential to move on quickly from a mistake or failure in order to project your confidence as a leader.

The World's Best have a short-term memory of their mistakes and failures, and a long-term memory of their successes.

All of us are in sales in some way and face daily rejection. The rejection might include someone saying no to your face or on the phone, a potential client or customer choosing a different project or service than yours, or perhaps a potential client not returning a phone call or text, essentially ignoring you. To thrive in sales, you must manage your response to failure—and self-compassion is a must-have trait in order to build your business according to your vision and realize your potential. No matter how talented you are or how amazing your product or service is, the reality is that not everyone will say yes and purchase from you. Remember: rejections are not about you—it may be the wrong time, or your product just isn't the right thing for the person. It's easy to have a fight-or-flight response to failure and react emotionally. But remember not to let your amygdala get hijacked; you want to stay in your prefrontal cortex by thinking rationally about the rejection, mistake, or failure.

When I teach elite athletes, entrepreneurs, salespeople, and leaders how to let go of their mistakes quickly, I talk about "Learn, Burn, & Return," a catchy strategy for their High Performance

Toolbox. You can use it anytime you are having difficulty letting go of a mistake or failure. Personally, I use Learn, Burn, & Return several times throughout my week. Here are a few "big" failures I had to deliberate to apply the concept to, reframing the learnings multiple times:

- When I wasn't authentic on stage during my first speaker showcase and tried to be someone I was not (wow, that was a rough day).

- When I was not renewed while working with a high-profile team (yikes, that one hurt, even though it had nothing to do with me).

- When I yelled at my son for no reason at all (man, the guilt that comes from that!).

Learn, Burn, & Return goes like this:

Learn – Consider what you learned from the mistake *objectively*. This means staying unemotional and focused on what you plan to do in the future, instead of what you did in the past. To do this, start a sentence with "Next time I will . . ." Think of what you learned in an objective, factual way, instead of a subjective, biased way, and avoid taking the mistake to heart. Remember: humans are meaning-making machines. We want to intentionally choose the meaning we attach to failure.

Let's apply "Learn" to two examples:

1. A prospective client doesn't return your call. After reflecting objectively on the message you left, you learn that you want to improve your energy when leaving messages, to ensure you don't sound desperate for the sale. You could learn by thinking, *Next time I leave a message, I will speak from a place of abundance, knowing good things are coming my way.*

GET GRITTY

GET PURPOSE

MASTER THOUGHTS

KNOW SELF

DOMINATE CONTROLLABLES

OWN THE MOMENT

CHOOSE EMOTIONS

OWN WHO YOU ARE

LIVE AND LET GO

COURAGE ZONE

2. Let's say you get super nervous during a presentation to a big client. If you were to sign this client, it would change your year dramatically! During the presentation, you show your nerves, and your voice cracks. You lose the client, and you know you felt as nervous as you did because you weren't prepared enough. You take a learning approach and reflect to yourself, *Next time, I will spend several more hours preparing, then remind myself I have what it takes! I will even try some power breathing before a presentation, to decrease my nerves.*

Burn – The next step after learning from the mistake is to burn it. By "burn it," I mean let it go. This step is important because you cannot think about two things at once; you cannot think about the mistake in the past and what you need to do in the present moment at the same time. The next time you make a mistake, say one of the following as you let it go:

- "Let it go!"

- "Flush it."

- "Move on."

- "Burn it."

You could also choose an action to symbolize letting the mistake go:

- Brushing down your arm with your opposite hand, as if you are brushing something away.

- Adjusting your clothing, to restore your sense of comfort.

- Shifting the way you are sitting or standing, signaling to yourself that you're ready to move on.

I find that if you use a phrase and an action together, the impact is more powerful. What burn phrase or action do you want to choose to let the mistake go?

Return – After you have learned and burned, it's important to keep your self-talk and body language confident. You "return" to thinking and feeling confident *despite* the mistake. Repeat one or more Power Phrases in your mind to ensure the mistake doesn't impact your confidence and belief in yourself. You might say to yourself one of the following:

- "I am confident."

- "I'll get it next time."

- "I am incredible at my work."

- "I will close the next one."

- "This is what I am meant to do."

You can use the Learn, Burn, & Return strategy any time you make a mistake at work, in your business, or with your family. You can also teach your team this strategy, reminding them to have a short-term memory of their mistakes and failures but a long-term memory of their successes.

Why Perfectionism is Your Worst Enemy

One of the key characteristics that separates great athletes, entrepreneurs, salespeople, and leaders from the rest is a burning desire to be at their best. High performers know they can continue to grow, learn, and develop, and this desire to be their best keeps them striving for more. That same desire, however, can result in negative tendencies that undermine performance, happiness, and grit.

GET GRITTY

GET PURPOSE

MASTER THOUGHTS

KNOW SELF

DOMINATE CONTROLLABLES

OWN THE MOMENT

CHOOSE EMOTIONS

OWN WHO YOU ARE

LIVE AND LET GO

COURAGE ZONE

There are two types of perfectionism: adaptive and maladaptive, or positive and negative. The adaptive form of perfectionism can provide the drive that leads to great achievement and striving for excellence in business and life. People who are adaptively perfectionistic work with intense effort and drive to reach their high standards. They have little self-criticism when they do not succeed. They take their mistakes in stride, remembering that no one is perfect. This type of perfectionism has been linked to high levels of well-being and health. In fact, many view this positive perfectionism as a desirable personality trait in leaders, team members, and employees—their high standards and motivation help them gain a competitive advantage.

The maladaptive, negative form of perfectionism, also called "self-critical perfectionism," can be damaging and stop you in your tracks. This type of perfectionism has high standards but high levels of self-criticism and even shame. This is one of the most common psychological issues that I deal with as a coach. This maladaptive form includes a tendency to avoid problems, work in isolation, procrastinate, and ruminate over past events and mistakes. It can cut your confidence and shred your self-esteem. You focus on avoiding failure instead of making things happen. You rarely feel good after a performance or at the end of your day, even if you gave your best effort. This negative form can kill the fun that drew you to your calling, your business, or your career path in the first place, leading to burnout, anxiety, and avoiding pressure situations. Maladaptive perfectionism is also related to lower work engagement as well as decreased life and job satisfaction.

One benefit of self-compassion is that it allows leaders to nurture adaptive, positive perfectionism. In fact, the research suggests that leaders that have high standards and practice self-compassion will be: (1) less likely to avoid or deny difficulties, (2) more likely to be creative and rational when experiencing problems, and (3) more likely to engage others when solving problems—which are all characteristics of a psychologically safe work culture.

Nearly every high-level athlete, entrepreneur, salesperson, and leader who I have worked with has perfectionistic tendencies. They have high standards, continuously give their best effort, and are driven to succeed. Their perfectionism got them where they are today. But individuals often come to me with many attributes of the negative, self-critical perfectionism.

For example, one vice president I work with used to feel the need to overprepare for presentations any time he felt as if he'd be evaluated. He would obsess over each detail, working long hours and evenings, sacrificing time with his young children and family. When he wouldn't excessively prepare, he would question his ability and knowledge—one time even experiencing an anxiety attack while presenting, even though he knew most of the people in the room. In our work together, we maintained the high standards he had for himself, but worked to modify his perfectionism toward the adaptive type. His happiness and balance between work and family improved, and the anxiety and pressure he felt decreased.

How do we keep perfectionism from sabotaging us and our business? Here are some ideas to get you started:

- **Strive for excellence over perfection** – Remind yourself to have self-compassion and that perfection is impossible. Striving for excellence is within your reach, while perfectionism is not.

- **"Done" is better than "perfect"** – It's easy to get stuck aiming for perfection in your business, but striving to be perfect keeps you spinning instead of moving on. Remember that you can always make changes as time goes on.

GET GRITTY

GET PURPOSE

MASTER THOUGHTS

KNOW SELF

DOMINATE CONTROLLABLES

OWN THE MOMENT

CHOOSE EMOTIONS

OWN WHO YOU ARE

LIVE AND LET GO

COURAGE ZONE

- **Embrace obstacles** – One thing is certain: you will experience obstacles and setbacks while building your business to your bold vision. A maladaptive perfectionist might give up, viewing obstacles as failure. Stay the course, keep pivoting, and adjust as necessary, tapping into your creativity along the way.

- **Focus on why you do what you do** – The maladaptive form of perfectionism can be accompanied by an intense concern over the opinions of others (bosses, colleagues, friends, etc.) or the worry that you may let them down. Instead, push aside those worrisome thoughts by focusing on what you think about yourself and why you love what you do.

As a top-performing business leader, entrepreneur, or salesperson, it is good to strive for success and have high expectations. These high standards keep you going, striving to be your best. When you strive to be your best, you help others around you do the same. But perfection is unattainable. Instead, consider taking your mistakes in stride—remember, no one is perfect. Moving on quickly—reminding yourself to "Learn, Burn, & Return"—will protect your confidence, motivation, and vision, enabling you to pursue your calling and purpose.

My High Performance Game Plan
LIVE AND LET GO

1. I commit to practicing daily self-compassion. I'll take a nonjudgmental approach to observing my negative emotions and thoughts.

2. I'll consider how I can create psychological safety in my business to enhance innovation and performance—but ultimately to help my team feel safe and supported in trying new things.

3. When I have difficulty moving on from a mistake, I'll remember to Learn, Burn, & Return and teach my team to do the same.

4. I will continue to have high standards for my work and the work of others, striving for excellence over perfection.

Now, take a moment to record the following on your Grit Board:

- Your definition of *failure*

- Your commitment to creating a psychologically safe team

- A few key phrases such as "Learn, Burn, & Return"; "Be Self-Compassionate"; or "Choose Excellence over Perfection."

My High Performance Power Phrase:

I see failure and mistakes as opportunities to learn and grow. When I fail, I take an easygoing approach. I remember to Learn, Burn, & Return.

10

Choose Your Courage Zone

The World's Best

feel uncomfortable regularly. Staying in your
Comfort Zone inhibits growth.
High performers know that
magic happens in their Courage Zone.

Choose Your Courage Zone

"Risk more than others think is safe.
Dream more than others think is practical."
—Howard Schultz, CEO of Starbucks

---

ark Davis has made a tradition of being entrepreneurial, following in his father's footsteps and encouraging his children to follow in his. His father, Stan, started St. Peter Creamery in 1943, selling butter to the US government during World War II. Mark started as a can truck driver in the company, and then during college became a semi milk truck driver. In the 1970s, taking over management, he toured several factories and suppliers in Europe with a group of US dairy processing managers. As a result, Mark and the family made several decisions that greatly impacted the future of the company, later named Davisco Foods International. He'd noticed America's growing appetite for cheese, so they started shifting the company to focus on producing cheese, eventually becoming one of Kraft's largest suppliers of cheese.

In 1982, with innovation top of mind, Mark and the family decided to mortgage the company—worth $3 million at the time—to purchase bioseparation technology for the development of high-protein whey, a risky decision because few companies were manufacturing whey. Davisco became one of the first producers of high-protein whey, now under the brand BiPro. To keep up with the demand, he reinvested resources and opened more factories across the country. His children worked in the factories and went to college, furthering their knowledge of dairy processing and new products, bringing back new skill sets, and working in various leadership roles to keep the company growing and innovating. Mark and his family eventually grew Davisco to a $1.1 billion dairy operation.

When I interviewed Mark for the book, I asked him if he'd ever feared he was making the wrong decision. He replied, "I never had the feeling of fear, just that it could be done." As we talked about mistakes, he shared one "mistake" that became a game changer for the Davis family:

One day, his son Marty came to him suggesting that he invest money into a quartz company. He followed his son's suggestion, but shortly after the investment, the quartz company went bankrupt. The Davis family had the opportunity to purchase the company at an acquisition and did so despite the risk at the time. The quartz company, which you may now know as Cambria, cost roughly $8 million to purchase and $36 million to get up and running. Cambria didn't turn a profit for the first five years.

Marty, who is now the CEO of Cambria, said in a newspaper interview, "We had no money. We were losing $600,000 to $700,000 a month. We were borrowed to the hilt and we were running out of runway." At the time, Mark decided to partner with radio commentator Paul Harvey in a celebrity advertising contract, which helped turn things around. Cambria is now estimated as a $250 million-a-year business. Mark concluded, "Investing in the company at the beginning might have been seen as a mistake by some, but there are always possibilities in mistakes."

GET GRITTY

GET PURPOSE

MASTER THOUGHTS

KNOW SELF

DOMINATE CONTROLLABLES

OWN THE MOMENT

CHOOSE EMOTIONS

OWN WHO YOU ARE

LIVE AND LET GO

COURAGE ZONE

Mark Davis, now the CEO of Davis Holdings, took calculated risks that paid off. In 2012, he sold to his family, who eventually separated the holdings and sold Davisco Foods International to Canadian firm Agropur in July 2014 for an undisclosed sum. The Davis family also bought and sold Sun Country Airlines in 2011 and 2017, respectively. According to Mark, the key to their family's success was the risks they took. "My dad learned to take risks that others weren't willing to take," he said. "We followed his lead."

Choose Courage over Comfort

Our daily activities can be divided into two zones: our Courage Zone and our Comfort Zone. When we are in our Comfort Zone, we do not grow. We play small and live small. We dream small. We just survive, settle for less, and are okay with being like everyone else. In our Comfort Zone, we engage in activities that make us feel good, instead of activities that will move the needle in our business. We avoid confrontation, tension, and difficult conversations. We let fear, doubt, regret, and insecurity get the best of us, resulting in mediocrity. Many people live in their Comfort Zone—but not intentional leaders, high performers, or business owners who are making their dreams happen! Not you!

<u>COURAGE</u>
COMFORT

It's comfortable to stay comfortable—it feels good and safe. But what if I told you that the *only way* to make your vision for your business a reality is to get uncomfortable each and every day, and that the more uncomfortable you are each day, the more quickly your vision will become reality. The *only way* you can reach the people you are intended to serve in this world is to get uncomfortable! Read that again and let it sink in. You can't choose both courage *and* comfort—it's either courage *or* comfort.

If you want to step into your destiny and reach your bold vision, become the best leader you can, live a life of meaning and significance, and build your business into a massive success, getting uncomfortable daily is a necessity. Discomfort is the price you pay to step into your destiny, live a meaningful life, and experience success. Feeling discomfort daily is a prerequisite—necessary for you to reach the vision you outlined. Getting comfortable being uncomfortable *daily* is a must for you to make the impact you are meant to make.

High performers, successful salespeople, and business owners who are crushing it choose activities in their Courage Zone each day. The reason growth happens so fast in your Courage Zone is because you are developing and expanding yourself. You're trying new things, connecting with new clients, building relationships, having difficult conversations, talking in front of large groups, and conquering your fears, acting with courage and bravery. You're taking calculated risks—turning "impossible" into "I'm possible"—and pursuing your big, bold, audacious dreams.

The Courage Zone is a place of self-discovery, growth, and—yes—failure. But the more you fail, the quicker you succeed. You "learn and burn," finding out more quickly what works and what doesn't work. Your Courage Zone is where you realize your potential, and it is the only place you can reach high performance and your bold vision. Courage is not the absence of fear or discomfort; it is the ability to move toward the fear and discomfort regardless of how you feel. Courage is the ability to do what is scary! You can develop skills to help you choose courage over comfort, and that is what this chapter is all about.

GET GRITTY

GET PURPOSE

MASTER THOUGHTS

KNOW SELF

DOMINATE CONTROLLABLES

OWN THE MOMENT

CHOOSE EMOTIONS

OWN WHO YOU ARE

LIVE AND LET GO

COURAGE ZONE

> *"Courage is not the absence of fear, but rather the assessment that something else is more important than the fear."*—FRANKLIN D. ROOSEVELT

To step into your Courage Zone each day—a key practice in your success—ask yourself this powerful question each morning:

What do I need to do today that is uncomfortable?

Here are some of my clients' responses to that question:

- "Decide on a new way of marketing the business."

- "Cold-call a client I want to work with."

- "Give difficult feedback to an employee."

- "Plan my calendar down to fifteen-minute increments."

- "Post a video on social media."

- "Personally get to know someone I lead."

- "Delegate tasks to an employee or assistant."

- "Take out a loan to develop a new product."

- "Speak in front of or be vulnerable with my employees."

- "Fire or have a courageous conversation with an employee."

- "Pivot the business in a new direction."

So each morning—perhaps as part of your GRIT Morning

Routine—ask yourself, *What do I need to do today that is uncomfortable?* So you don't forget to ask yourself this powerful question each day, you could write it on a sticky note, then place it by your computer or alarm clock, or you could snap a pic and set it as the background image on your phone. When you remind yourself of this each day and commit to doing one thing that is uncomfortable or a little scary, you step into your destiny. You call the person you need to, try a new idea or strategy, or speak your mind. These small courageous changes lead to big results, and the big results lead you to your vision!

Risk-Taking Is Key

Richard Branson—billionaire, adventurer, and founder of the ever-expanding Virgin Group—experienced success because he took bold risks, as he describes in his book *Finding My Virginity.* He founded the Virgin brand in 1970, and Virgin Group now comprises more than thirty-five companies and sixty thousand employees worldwide. Branson has said he loves both challenge and venturing into new areas of business—the combination having led him to build his net worth to more than $4 billion. He was knighted by the British government for his services in entrepreneurship and the impact he has had on the world.

Branson has experienced big failures along the way, but he's continued adapting to changing circumstances by pivoting and adjusting—the mark of a successful entrepreneur, as we have discussed in this book. For example, in 1967, Branson dropped out of school at age sixteen to start his first business, *Student* magazine. The magazine provided a voice to the youth of the time, but it made little profit. Instead of going under, he pivoted, launching a mail-order discount-record business as a way to grow the magazine. This mail-order business later became Virgin Records, which grew into a billion-dollar recording empire.

Branson said, "Don't let the fear of failure become an obstacle.

GET GRITTY

GET PURPOSE

MASTER THOUGHTS

KNOW SELF

DOMINATE CONTROLLABLES

OWN THE MOMENT

CHOOSE EMOTIONS

OWN WHO YOU ARE

LIVE AND LET GO

COURAGE ZONE

Entrepreneurship in its very essence is all about taking risks. You can create your own luck by opening the door to change. If every entrepreneur—including myself—feared failure, then few companies would ever have seen progress or success. No one ever reached the stars from the comfort of their couch!" Branson is now one of the most influential businesspeople on the planet—which wouldn't have happened without his ability to take bold risks and move past fear or discomfort.

Courage and risk-taking are key factors in experiencing success in both your personal life and your business. It is difficult, even impossible, to build your business without risking something—be it your reputation, your money, or even the failure of your business. Risk-taking is necessary and inherent in business because there is no guarantee that you will succeed.

Some research suggests that entrepreneurs and business leaders are more prone to risk and have a more positive attitude about it than those who choose not to be entrepreneurs and business leaders. Business owners who take risks are more innovative, flexible, and open to new opportunities. According to German researchers who surveyed more than twenty thousand people, those who enjoy taking risks also reported more satisfaction in their lives and more contentment in their lives and businesses. Improving your risk-taking tolerance is key to building your business toward your bold vision.

For example, consider the following entrepreneurs, leaders, and business owners who took risks that paid off:

- Arianna Huffington, founder of the *Huffington Post*, was discouraged to start a new publication by her family, but she put in the hard work to gain investor buy-in to make it successful. She said that the most important lesson for an entrepreneur is that "Failure is not the opposite of success—it is a stepping stone for success."

- Oprah Winfrey, who is one of the most successful women entrepreneurs in the world, risked her financial security by signing a deal for her own television program. *The Oprah Winfrey Show* became the highest-rated program of its kind. After growing up in poverty and becoming pregnant at the age of fourteen, she went on to become the only African American woman on the Forbes Billionaires list. She said, "Do the one thing you think you cannot do. Fail at it. Try again. Do better the second time. The only people who never tumble are those who never mount the high wire."

- Jeff Bezos was a senior vice president of a hedge fund on Wall Street when he felt a calling to become an entrepreneur. He left the security of his job to start Amazon in his garage in 1994. He is now the wealthiest man in the world, and Amazon is *the* go-to online store for just about everything. Bezos said, "I projected myself forward to age eighty. I don't want to be eighty years old, cataloging a bunch of major regrets of my life." This practice of future casting gave him the passion to go for it, showing us that taking a leap of faith can pay off.

GET GRITTY

GET PURPOSE

MASTER THOUGHTS

KNOW SELF

DOMINATE CONTROLLABLES

OWN THE MOMENT

CHOOSE EMOTIONS

OWN WHO YOU ARE

LIVE AND LET GO

COURAGE ZONE

None of these entrepreneurs just rolled the dice and went for it. They all took calculated risks—they were prepared, did their research, and made informed decisions. As entrepreneurs and business leaders, we can be overly optimistic and overconfident, forming a positive bias toward risk, which may make us too confident and too optimistic when making decisions in our business. In fact, there is some research to suggest that entrepreneurs tend to be more strongly focused on strengths and benefits than on weaknesses and threats while analyzing business decisions. This can get us into trouble if we aren't careful. I have to remind myself of this often! The key is to move forward taking *calculated risks*—having courage to be innovative at the same time as using the facts and numbers to make decisions. A word of caution: make sure to weigh your ratio of risks and benefits as you move toward your bold vision for your business. Do the research, set goals and checkpoints, and be willing to adjust and pivot along the way—that's what successful entrepreneurs do.

Challenge or Threat?

Many times we want to avoid stress and pressure, but avoiding both keeps us in our Comfort Zone. In fact, taking risks *requires* being courageous and feeling some stress and pressure. A key variable in your ability to take risks and be courageous is how you perceive threats, challenges, and opportunities.

I love Kelly McGonigal's book *The Upside of Stress* because it provides practical suggestions on how to see the good that can be created from stress and pressure, based on scientific research. Referring to decades of research, she said, "The latest science reveals that stress can make you smarter, stronger, and more successful. It helps you learn and grow. It can even inspire courage and compassion. The best way to manage stress isn't to reduce or avoid it, but rather to rethink and even embrace it."

A study of Navy SEAL candidates demonstrated results similar to the research McGonigal touched on in her book. When researchers followed 174 Navy SEAL candidates, they found that in the extreme setting they train and work in, believing stress was helpful predicted greater persistence, faster obstacle-course times, and fewer negative evaluations from peers and instructors. The key to viewing stress as enhancing our performance, compared to debilitating our performance, is all about our perspective and view of the situation.

If we see stress and pressure as threats as an entrepreneur, salesperson, or business owner, we stay in our Comfort Zone—dreaming small, questioning our abilities, and holding ourselves back. Seeing difficulties as challenges, not threats, is key to our ability to move forward courageously. It's not about the reality of the situation you are in; instead, it's all about how you perceive the situation and what meaning you attach to it—comfort or courage.

We saw many businesses impacted by the COVID-19 pandemic. As a business owner or entrepreneur, if you saw COVID-19 as a threat to your business—to the factors you control, at least—you likely lacked the creativity, energy, and grit to pivot and adjust. But if you saw COVID-19 as a challenge, you likely stayed creative, willing to try new ways of marketing, new products, or new ideas about how to reach your prospective clients. This choice—seeing a difficulty as a threat or a challenge—predicts your business's success amid uncertainty.

When you see a difficulty as a *threat*, you believe you don't have enough resources to deal and cope with the situation. You believe the situation is too demanding, that you cannot handle what's going on. You feel the pressure and anxiety throughout your body, and your thinking isn't always rational or accurate.

GET GRITTY

GET PURPOSE

MASTER THOUGHTS

KNOW SELF

DOMINATE CONTROLLABLES

OWN THE MOMENT

CHOOSE EMOTIONS

OWN WHO YOU ARE

LIVE AND LET GO

COURAGE ZONE

On the other hand, when you see a difficulty as a *challenge*—that slight but powerful change in perspective—you want to go for it and conquer the challenge. Physically, you feel excited and fired up, with the right amount of adrenaline and energy, because you have interpreted the same signs—pounding heart, sweaty palms, and butterflies in your stomach—as helping you, not hindering you. You possess the confidence in yourself and your plan to overcome the challenge. You move forward courageously. You know you have enough resources in our business and within yourself to overcome and cope with the situation. Your focus is like a laser beam on the challenge in front of you. You increase your chances of success because you are seeing the situation as something you can overcome.

When you have a challenge mindset, instead of a threat mindset, you are talking to yourself powerfully to stay courageous. This can sound like the following:

- "I have the resources within me to handle this."

- "I can handle anything that comes my way."

- "I have everything I need inside me now."

When you feel those signs of anxiety—pounding heart, sweaty palms, and butterflies in your stomach—focus less on making them go away and more on interpreting them as signs you are ready for the challenge. When you feel anxiety or fear, it means that what you are doing is important to you. It means you need to move forward. You could say to yourself, *Okay, I know this is important to me* or, *I got this. I just know this means I care.*

Embrace the energy you feel to fuel your performance.

Focus more on how you can use that energy to rise to the challenge. You might think that top performers such as pro athletes, surgeons, and musicians are always calm under pressure, but they're actually using a challenge mindset to give themselves access to the mental and physical resources they need to rise to the occasion. A challenge mindset helps the Word's Best achieve high performance.

Say Hello to Fear

All of my executive coaching clients experience fear while pushing hard and staying gritty about their goals and dreams, and most of them need some one-on-one coaching to address fear specifically. That's because fear applies to all of us. We can't grow toward the person we are meant to become without fear. My clients' fear has manifested in the following ways:

- Having a goal of making $1 million dollars in their business, but fearing asking for the referrals to grow their business.

- Wanting to hire their first employee or grow their team, but fearing they won't make enough revenue to pay for it.

- Desiring to write a book, but fearing that no one will read it, making them want to give up.

- Knowing deep down they want to start their own business, but fearing the loss of a full-time salary at their current job.

- Wanting to speak their mind more at work or with leadership, but fearing no one will listen or they won't be taken seriously.

- Knowing it's their calling to start a podcast or get out in the world with their message, but fearing what others will think.

GET GRITTY

GET PURPOSE

MASTER THOUGHTS

KNOW SELF

DOMINATE CONTROLLABLES

OWN THE MOMENT

CHOOSE EMOTIONS

OWN WHO YOU ARE

LIVE AND LET GO

COURAGE ZONE

Can you hear yourself in any of these examples? What do you fear? As you continue to choose courage over comfort and step into your bold vision, it's helpful to understand fear and the 8 Fear Facts. Let's dive in.

Fear Fact 1: Fear applies to all of us – Fear is universal but also very personal. We can fear pain, difficulty, embarrassment, rejection, outcome, the unknown, loneliness, and lack of control, among other things. We all experience fear. However, what I fear might be different than what you fear. Each of us has our own unique Comfort Zone, just one of many ways we are different from one another.

Fear Fact 2: Fear lives in the future – When we feel fear, our focus is on the future. We can't experience fear when reflecting on the past or when our mind is focused in the present. Fear is a future-based emotion, and you are likely imagining a worst-case scenario when you feel fear. We are at our best and experience the highest performance in the present moment, and fear takes us out of that.

Fear Fact 3: Everything you fear is self-created – Whenever you are trying something new, taking on a new project, going after a new goal, or stretching yourself emotionally or physically in some way, you will experience fear. You might fear pivoting your business, trying a new way of marketing, or asking for a referral to keep growing your business. The very thing you fear can provide you with your greatest growth experience. Doing what is scary will allow you to address your fear.

Fear Fact 4: We cannot eliminate fear, nor should we – Fear keeps us safe; it is part of what makes us human. Fear helps us make good decisions about our business, health, and safety. For example, when our son had COVID-19, at the beginning of the pandemic, fear kept us in our home and making good decisions about social distancing as a family. Fear of embarrassment can help you double-check that email before you send it off or help you stay gritty when your business is in a downturn. Your goal should not be to eliminate fear but to address the fears that hold you back, making a choice to be courageous despite the fear.

Fear Fact 5: Courage is feeling the fear and walking into it – Courage is not the absence of fear. In fact, you can't feel courage without fear; you need fear in order to act in a courageous way. The goal is not to be *fearless*, completely lacking fear; instead, the goal is to *fear less*. Fears will be there as you continue to build your business and take courageous actions. Being courageous means that you have the bravery to move toward the fear and step into it.

Fear Fact 6: We must choose courage over fear to reach our potential – I had one of my "grit sisters," Shannon Polson—author of *The Grit Factor* and founder of The Grit Institute—on the *High Performance Mindset* podcast, episode 354. Shannon was also one of the first female Apache-helicopter pilots. On the episode, Shannon shared that fear is a form of resistance, that when you are flying an Apache helicopter, you don't avoid the wind—you fly into it. Fly into your fear, my friends, because the real enemy to your success is not fear—it is comfort.

Fear Fact 7: One way to move forward despite fear is to take the next step that aligns with your values – What values are important to you and your leadership, and how could you use them to take courageous action? What is the next step toward making that happen? How is courage needed to take that next step? For example, if one of your values is "service," your next step is to take an action that best serves your client. Perhaps that next step, for example, is to post an educational video on social media that helps your ideal client to pick up the phone and have a courageous conversation or to design a new product that best serves their clients. You cannot share your message and/or the value of your product and how it helps people without courage. You need courage to take action, and it is easier when the action is aligned with your values.

Discomfort is the price you pay to step into your destiny, live a meaningful life, and experience success.

Fear Fact 8: We must do the thing that we fear to serve those we are intended to serve – The *only way* you can reach the people you are intended to serve in this world is to get uncomfortable! To reach high performance, you must do what scares you. Fear can paralyze you if you let it. It is a four-letter word that can be harmful to our grit, happiness, and performance. Some people let fear stop them from taking the necessary steps toward achieving their goals and dreams. But not you. You think and act like the World's Best. The World's Best choose courage instead of fear. They feel the fear, but don't let it keep them from doing what they want to, have to, or were designed to do. High performers know that when they feel fear, it means they are doing something important and meaningful.

Dreams That Are Scary

A few years ago, I was asked to come speak to a classroom of fifth graders. I'd been writing monthly newspaper articles, and this class had been reading and discussing them regularly. (It's great that they were being exposed to mindset training so early!) They asked me every question under the sun, and it was such a fun experience overall.

Toward the end of my time with the students, the teacher asked me a question I won't forget: "Cindra, what is your favorite quote?" Boldly and courageously, I said, "If your dreams do not scare you, they are not big enough." I had been using that quote by Ellen Johnson Sirleaf—who served as president of Liberia and became the first woman to lead an African nation—to help me embrace my own bold vision and push myself into courageous action each day. The teacher was shocked and almost fell off her chair! In front of the fifth graders, she said, "Cindra, why in the world should your dreams be scary?" I said, "Your dreams should be just outside your Comfort Zone, because then you are always growing and expanding yourself. Dreams help you be all that you can be, and if you aren't dreaming big, you are playing small with your life." I could tell by the glossy look in her eyes that she wasn't paying attention during the next ten minutes, as we wrapped up.

Afterward, she came up to me privately and said, "I just had an aha moment. Thank you so much for saying that quote, Cindra. I realized at that moment that I didn't have any dreams. I've been doing this job for thirty years, and I forgot to keep dreaming."

"The size of your dreams must always exceed your current capacity to achieve them. If your dreams do not scare you, they are not big enough."
—Ellen Johnson Sirleaf

It's easy to experience life as this teacher did for so many years—in her Comfort Zone and not pushing herself to dream a little bigger. Goals and dreams are inside us to help us step into all that we can become. Setting goals is less about checking off a box and more about who we become by pushing toward our big dream and vision. When you dream big, you are more

GET GRITTY

GET PURPOSE

MASTER THOUGHTS

KNOW SELF

DOMINATE CONTROLLABLES

OWN THE MOMENT

CHOOSE EMOTIONS

OWN WHO YOU ARE

LIVE AND LET GO

COURAGE ZONE

likely to reach your full potential because you are growing and expanding yourself each day. So, my friends, as we wrap up the book, consider these questions:

What are your scary dreams? Could you level up the scariness of those dreams just a little?

As you consider what your scary dreams are, write them down (or even draw them) so you can keep a record, and check in on your scary dreams often. When you write down your dreams, your brain works on them subconsciously. Most people dream too small, often letting their limiting beliefs get in the way. But when we push ourselves to dream one notch more than we normally would, we grow. Dreaming above your Comfort Zone requires you to consider all the possibilities and to choose courage over comfort. You might hear that your dreams are unrealistic or impossible. Choose not to listen! You know in your heart that your dreams can and will happen!

Your Courage Map

Last year, I attended a speaking event where I heard John C. Maxwell—speaker, coach, and New York Times bestselling author who has sold more than twenty-four million books in fifty languages, including *The 21 Irrefutable Laws of Leadership* and *How Successful People Think*—share his thoughts on courage, and I've summarized them below, adding some of my own thoughts on the topic:

- Courage is practiced by you—no one else can practice it for you.

- Courage is a decision powered by your decision to feed it.

- Courage grows by exercising it.

- Courage is used—it cannot be stored.

- Courage is faith in the future.

- Courage keeps you going and also allows you to begin.

- Courage is born when you tap into your values.

- Courage is fueled by empowering emotions such as optimism, hope, confidence, and, especially, gratitude.

To help you consider how you can have more courage in your life and business, consider five fears that hold you back. Perhaps you fear that your business will fail, or that you won't reach your goals, or that other people will have bad opinions of you, or that you'll get to the end of your life and feel regret. Write out your five fears as "What if . . ." statements as part of the exercise below. Then, answer each "What if . . ." statement with a "Then I will . . ." statement to help you move beyond the fear. It is easier to choose courage when you have a plan to address the fear.

Courage Map Examples:

- **What if** the person I call hangs up the phone on me or is not interested in my product? **Then I will** call the next person on my list.

- **What if** I don't reach my financial goals at the end of the year? **Then I will** pivot and adjust and continue to move new projects forward to make more profit.

- **What if** the product I am designing doesn't make the impact I think it can? **Then I will** stay creative and innovative, encouraging myself and my team to focus on our next product.

GET GRITTY

GET PURPOSE

MASTER THOUGHTS

KNOW SELF

DOMINATE CONTROLLABLES

OWN THE MOMENT

CHOOSE EMOTIONS

OWN WHO YOU ARE

LIVE AND LET GO

COURAGE ZONE

Now you try.

Courage Up 7-Day Challenge

Moving out of your Comfort Zone and into your Courage Zone takes only a moment! Remember that courage is not the absence of fear or doubt, but it *is* the ability to do something that is scary. You can train your mind to act more courageously every day. One way to do that is to take the Courage Up 7-Day Challenge. This challenge is inspired by this quote by Eleanor Roosevelt:

"Do one thing every day that scares you. Those small things that make us uncomfortable help us build the courage to do the work we do."

Committing to one thing that is uncomfortable or a little scary each day helps you live your purpose, reach your big vision, serve your intended clients, and stay gritty in the process. I like starting with only seven days because the short time frame is highly achievable. When those seven days are over, start again on your next seven day challenge. This could be calling the person you need to, speaking in front of a group, being vulnerable with your employees by sharing more about you and your passion, or starting a new division of the company. Only you determine what is scary for you! Small changes lead to big results.

Make doing something a little scary—choosing courage over comfort—a daily habit. Recently, I read *Tiny Habits: The Small Changes That Change Everything*, written by BJ Fogg, a Stanford researcher and director of the Behavior Design Lab. That book introduced me to two big ideas related to how we can make choosing courage a daily habit:

The first big idea is his Fogg Behavior Model—abbreviated as "B=MAP"—which states that a Behavior requires Motivation, Ability, and a Prompt to converge at the same moment. To ensure you follow through with your new habit of choosing something courageous each day, you'll want to make sure your motivation is high. To determine your current level of motivation, consider the following:

- What good will choosing courage each day do for your business and those clients or customers you serve?

- How can you change their lives or have a big impact?

- Why is choosing courage each day necessary for you to reach your bold vision?

- How can you make choosing courage over comfort easy each day?

The second big idea I learned from Fogg is to celebrate your habits each time you follow through—in this case, celebrate each time you show courage. When you celebrate, your brain experiences a hit of dopamine. Fogg describes this celebration as "shine" and suggests we use those emotions to create habits. He asks you to consider how you would celebrate if your favorite team came from behind to win at the last minute, then reinforce your courageous habits with that same natural celebration—arms in the air, fist pumps, congratulatory yells, etc. Allow yourself to feel successful after you have taken the courageous step, regardless of the result. This makes the courageous behavior more automatic, and the celebration helps you handle the failure. Allow yourself to celebrate the small things, because small, courageous actions change everything! Each morning I got up to write this book, I gave myself a pump of my arm, as I would when my favorite NFL team wins at the last minute. It helped create the habit that resulted in this book!

GET GRITTY

GET PURPOSE

MASTER THOUGHTS

KNOW SELF

DOMINATE CONTROLLABLES

OWN THE MOMENT

CHOOSE EMOTIONS

OWN WHO YOU ARE

LIVE AND LET GO

COURAGE ZONE

Don't settle for mediocrity or regrets because you are scared to step out of your Comfort Zone. Choose to step into your Courage Zone each day—make it a habit! See choosing uncomfortable things as adventurous and exciting, not scary or nerve-racking. As children, we are natural risk takers, but as we grow, we hold back and attempt fewer things. Live life like a child, and, as Nike says, "Just do it!" When you step outside your Comfort Zone, you are creating who you will become. You are creating your future self—and your future self needs courage!

Take the leap and accept the Courage Up 7-Day Challenge. To do so, each day this week, commit to doing something that is uncomfortable and scary. Each day, do at least one thing in your Courage Zone. This will help you more quickly make your vision a reality and serve those you are intended to serve. Then, when you are done with those seven days, start another Courage Up 7-Day Challenge. Continue like that until doing something scary each day becomes part of who you are and how you live your life!

My High Performance Game Plan
CHOOSE YOUR COURAGE ZONE

1. I commit to doing one thing in my Courage Zone each day to more quickly make my vision a reality and serve those I am intended to serve. The question "What do I need to do *today* that is uncomfortable?" will guide me.

2. I choose courage each day, remembering that it is the price I pay for stepping into my destiny, living a meaningful life, and experiencing success.

3. Next time I am overcome by fear, I will remember the 8 Fear Facts, including that fear applies to everyone and that I can step into my fear by reminding myself of my values.

4. To get clear on my fears, I will use the Courage Map, considering "What if . . ." and "Then I will . . ." to ignite my courage and reduce my fear.

Now, take a moment to record the following on your Grit Board:

- The courage question: "What do I need to do *today* that is uncomfortable?"

- Two or three scary dreams

- A few key phrases such as "Courage over comfort"; "See difficulties as challenges, not threats"; "What if . . . Then I will . . ."; or "My dreams scare me."

My High Performance Power Phrase:
I choose courage over fear.
I flex my courage muscle and go for it.

The
Beyond
Grit

I AM GRITTY.

I AM PASSIONATE and have a **CLEAR VISION** of the life I am building.

I own my purpose.

I talk to myself, not just listen.

I DOMINATE THE CONTROLLABLES.

I KNOW MY REASON FOR BEING AND LIVE MY PURPOSE EACH DAY.

I own the moment.

I SEE THE OPPORTUNITY IN EVERY DIFFICULTY.

I choose to lead the hardest person first— **myself.**

I CHOOSE TO RESPOND WITH **PURPOSE & INTENTION.**

I Learn, Burn, & Return.

I take **100% responsibility** for my success.

I CAN DO ANYTHING AND BE ANYTHING—
RIGHT HERE, RIGHT NOW.

I choose positivity.

The world needs me and my gifts.

I choose to bring an **OPTIMISTIC PERSPECTIVE** each day, looking for the opportunity.

→ **I WILL SHOW** ←
MY AUTHENTIC SELF
TO THE WORLD TODAY.

I TAKE AN EASYGOING APPROACH WHEN I FAIL.

I see failure and mistakes as **OPPORTUNITIES** *to learn and grow.*

I choose COURAGE over fear.

I FLEX MY COURAGE MUSCLE AND **GO FOR IT.**

Free Resources to Go Beyond Grit in Your Business

Here you are, at the end of this book, with ten new practices and a mindset to help you realize your potential and soar as an entrepreneur, business leader, or salesperson.

This book provides strategies and tools to help you develop a High Performance Mindset, enabling you to go after your bold, courageous vision and realize your potential. I created the Beyond Grit Leadership Manifesto (previous pages) to provide you with a visual reminder of all you learned in this book. Print it out, and post it as a visual reminder of going Beyond Grit.

To help you apply the information provided, I've created bonuses for you at beyondgrit.com/bonus. There, you'll find all the resources I referred to in this book, including the GRIT Morning Routine, Grit Values Exercise, Grit Meditation, and so much more. And you can take the Beyond Grit Questionnaire to find out how you score on the Top 10 Practices of the World's Best. You can find more information about the *Beyond Grit Workbook* and *Beyond Grit Cards* at **cindrakamphoff.com**.

There, you can also sign up to get regular emails with tools and strategies to go Beyond Grit or be updated about when my next book is released. Your email address will never be shared, and you can unsubscribe at any time.

Word of mouth is crucial for any author to succeed. If you enjoyed this book, please consider leaving an online review, even if it's just a line or two. Your review would make all the difference in the world! I am grateful for you!

Finally, I am here to help. For more information about having me come speak to or coach you or your team, you can reach me at (507) 327-9193 or cindra@cindrakamphoff. com. Please share your ideas, feedback, and questions by emailing me at the above address or finding me on Instagram at @CindraKamphoff. Share a picture of your Grit Board— I'd love to see it!

The next level is calling you.
Stay gritty and mentally strong, my friend!

Book's website: beyondgrit.com

Author's website: cindrakamphoff.com

LinkedIn and Instragram: @CindraKamphoff

Twitter: @Mentally_Strong

Facebook: @drcindrakamphoff

Email: cindra@cindrakamphoff.com

Podcast: cindrakamphoff.com/podcast

References

Introduction

Bryant, Andrew, and Ana Lucia Kazan. *Self-Leadership: How to Become a More Successful, Efficient, and Effective Leader from the Inside Out.* New York: McGraw Hill, 2012.

Enrod, Hal. *The Miracle Morning: The Not-So-Obvious Secret Guaranteed to Transform Your Life Before 8AM.* Miracle Morning Publishing, LLC, 2012.

Kamphoff, Cindra. *Beyond Grit: Ten Powerful Practices to Gain the High-Performance Edge.* Minneapolis: Wise Ink, 2017.

Kamphoff, Cindra. *Beyond Grit Workbook: Exercises to Gain the High-Performance Edge.* Minneapolis: Wise Ink, 2017.

Spall, Benjamin, and Michael Xander. *My Morning Routine: How Successful People Start Every Day Inspired.* New York: Portfolio, 2018.

Chapter 1

Duckworth, Angela. *Grit: The Power of Passion and Perseverance.* New York: Simon & Schuster, 2016.

Duckworth, Angela. "Grit: The Power of Passion and Perseverance." Filmed April 2013 at Ted Talks Education, New York, NY. https://www.ted.com/talks/angela_lee_duckworth_grit_the_power_of_passion_and_ perseverance.

Duckworth, Angela Lee, Patrick D. Quinn, and Martin E. P. Seligman. "Positive Predictors of Teacher Effectiveness." *The Journal of Positive Psychology* 4, no. 6 (2009): 540–47. https://doi.org/10.1080/1743976090315 7232.

Dugan, Riley, Bryan Hochstein, Maria Rouziou, and Benjamin Britton. "Gritting Their Teeth to Close the Sale: The Positive Effect of Salesperson Grit on Job Satisfaction and Performance." *Journal of Personal Selling & Sales Management* 39, no. 1 (2019): 81–101. https://doi.org/10.1080/08853134.2018.1489726.

Eskreis-Winkler, Lauren, Elizabeth P. Shulman, Scott A. Beal, and Angela L. Duckworth. "The Grit Effect: Predicting Retention in the Military, the Workplace, School and Marriage." *Frontiers in Psychology* 5 (2014): 36. https://doi.org/10.3389/fpsyg.2014.00036.

Fessler, Leah. "'You're No Genius': Her Father's Shutdowns Made Angela Duckworth a World Expert on Grit." *Quartz*, March 26, 2018. https://qz.com/work/1233940/angela-duckworth-explains-grit-is-the-key-to-success-and-self-confidence/.

Grosvenor, Edwin. "Sara Blakely, Shapewear." *Invention & Technology* 26, no. 1 (Winter 2020). https://www.inventionandtech.com/content/sara-blakely-shapewear.

Heekerens, Johannes Bodo, and Michael Eid. "Inducing Positive Affect and Positive Future Expectations Using the Best-Possible-Self Intervention: A Systematic Review and Meta-Analysis." *The Journal of Positive Psychology* 16, no. 3 (2021): 322–47. https://doi.org/10.1080/17439760.2020.1716052.

Hershfield, Hal E., and Daniel M. Bartels. "The Future Self." In *The Psychology of Thinking about the Future*, edited by Gabriele Oettingen, A. Timur Sevincer, and Peter M. Gollwitzer, 89–109. New York, NY: Guilford Press, 2018.

Hershfield, Hal E., Elicia M. John, and Joseph S. Reiff. "Using Vividness Interventions to Improve Financial Decision Making." *Policy Insights from the Behavioral and Brain Sciences* 5, no. 2 (2018): 209–15. https://doi.org/10.1177/2372732218787536.

Hershfield, Hal E. "How Can We Help Our Future Selves?" Filmed at TEDxEast. Uploaded September 9, 2014. YouTube. https://www.youtube.com/watch?v=tJotBbd7MwQ.

"How a Pitch in a Neiman Marcus Ladies Room Changed Sara Blakely's Life." *NPR*, September 12, 2016. https://www.npr.org/transcripts/493312213.

Kamphoff, Cindra, and Caroline Adams Miller. "418: Getting Grit with Caroline Adams Miller, Bestselling Author, Keynote Speaker and Educator." *High Performance Mindset*. Podcast, uploaded March 27, 2021. https://thehighperformancemindset.com/418-getting-grit -with-caroline-adams-miller-bestselling-author-keynote-speaker -and-educator.

Katie, Byron, and Stephen Mitchell. *Loving What Is: Four Questions That Can Change Your Life*. New York: Three Rivers Press, 2003.

Locke, Edwin A., and Gary P. Latham. "Building a Practically Useful Theory of Goal Setting and Task Motivation: A 35-Year Odyssey." *American Psychologist* 57, no. 9 (2002): 705–17. https:// doi.org/10.1037/0003-066X.57.9.705.

Locke, Edwin A., and Gary P. Latham. "New Directions in Goal-Setting Theory." *Current Directions in Psychological Science* 15, no. 5 (2006). https://doi.org/10.1111/j.1467-8721.2006.00449.x.

Martin, Jeffrey J., Brigid Byrd, Michele Lewis Watts, and Maana Dent. "Gritty, Hardy, and Resilient: Predictors of Sport Engagement and Life Satisfaction in Wheelchair Basketball Players." *Journal of Clinical Sport Psychology* 9, no. 4 (2015): 345–59.

Miller, Caroline Adams. *Getting Grit: The Evidence-Based Approach to Cultivating Passion, Perseverance, and Purpose*. Louisville, CO: Sounds True, 2017.

O'Connor, Clare. "How Sara Blakely of Spanx Turned $5,000 into $1 Billion." *Forbes*, March 14, 2012. https://www.forbes.com/global/2012/0326/billionaires -12-feature-united-states-spanx-sara-blakely-american-booty .html?sh=20eb05bd7ea0.

Polson, Shannon Huffman. *The Grit Factor: Courage, Resilience, and Leadership in the Most Male-Dominated Organization in the World*. New York: Harvard Business Review Press, 2020.

Rodriguez, Michael, Stefanie Boyer, David Fleming, and Scott Cohen. "Managing the Next Generation of Sales, Gen Z/Millennial Cusp: An Exploration of Grit, Entrepreneurship, and Loyalty." *Journal of Business-to-Business Marketing* 26, no. 1 (2019): 43–55. https://doi.org /10.1080/1051712X.2019.1565136.

Segal, Gillian Zoe. "This Self-Made Billionaire Failed the LSAT Twice, Then Sold Fax Machines for 7 Years before Hitting Big—Here's How She Got There." *CNBC*, April 3, 2019. https://www.cnbc.com/2019/04/03/self-made-billionaire-spanx-founder-sara-blakely-sold-fax-machines-before-making-it-big.html.

Schimschal, Sarah E. "Gritty Leaders: The Impact of Grit on Positive Leadership Capacity." *Psychological Reports* 122, no. 4 (2019): 1449–70. https://doi.org/10.1177/0033294118785547.

Von Culin, Katherine R., Eli Tsukayama, and Angela L. Duckworth. "Unpacking Grit: Motivational Correlates of Perseverance and Passion for Long-Term Goals." *The Journal of Positive Psychology* 9, no. 4 (2014): 306–12, https://doi.org/10.1080/17439760.2014.898320.

Wolters, Christopher A., and Maryam Hussain. "Investigating Grit and Its Relations with College Students' Self-Regulated Learning and Academic Achievement." *Metacognition and Learning* 10 (2015): 293–311. https://doi.org/10.1007/s11409-014-9128-9.

Chapter 2

Brown, Brené. *Daring Greatly: How the Courage to Be Vulnerable Transforms the Way We Live, Love, Parent, and Lead*. New York: Avery, 2012.

Covey, Stephen R. *The 7 Habits of Highly Effective People: 30th Anniversary Edition*. New York: Simon & Schuster, 2020.

Csikszentmihalyi, Mihaly. *Flow: The Psychology of Optimal Experience*. New York: Harper Collins, 1990.

Frankl, Viktor. *Man's Search for Meaning*. Boston: Beacon Press, 2006.

Kamphoff, Cindra, and Angie Bastian. "8: Turning a Single Kernel into an International Success with Angie's BOOMCHICKAPOP." *High Performance Mindset*. Podcast, uploaded September 18, 2015 https://thehighperformancemindset.com/transforming-a-kernel-of-an-idea-into-one-of-the-fastest-growing-popcorn-brands-angie-bastians-boomchickapop-talks-mindset-and-entrepreneurship.

Kamphoff, Cindra, and Richard Leider. "333: The Power of Purpose with Richard Leider, Bestselling Author & Keynote Speaker." *High Performance Mindset*. Podcast, uploaded May 2, 2020. https://thehighperformancemindset.com/333-the-power-of-purpose-with-richard-leider-bestselling-author-keynote-speaker.

García, Héctor, and Francesc Miralles. *Ikigai: The Japanese Secret to a Long and Happy Life*. London: Penguin Life, 2017.

Greenleaf Center for Servant Leadership. "The Servant as Leader." Accessed August 1, 2021. https://www.greenleaf.org/what-is-servant-leadership/.

Hendricks, Gay. *The Big Leap: Conquer Your Hidden Fear and Take Life to the Next Level*. New York: Harper Collins, 2009.

Houltberg, Benjamin J., Kenneth T. Wang, Wei Qi, and Christina S. Nelson. "Self-Narrative Profiles of Elite Athletes and Comparisons on Psychological Well-Being." *Research Quarterly for Exercise and Sport* 89, no. 3 (2018): 354–60, https://doi.org/10.1080/02701367.2018.1481919.

Leider, Richard J. *The Power of Purpose: Find Meaning, Live Longer, Better*. San Francisco, CA: Berrett-Koehler, 2010.

Sinek, Simon. *Start with Why: How Great Leaders Inspire Everyone to Take Action*. New York: Portfolio, 2011.

Chapter 3

Amen, Daniel G. *Change Your Brain, Change Your Life: The Breakthrough Program for Conquering Anxiety, Depression, Obsessiveness, Anger, and Impulsiveness*. New York: Three Rivers, 1998.

Bandura, A. "Self-Efficacy Mechanism in Human Agency." *American Psychologist* 37, no. 2 (1982): 122–47. https://doi.org/10.1037/0003-066X.37.2.122.

Hanson, Rick. *Hardwiring Happiness: The New Brain Science of Contentment, Calm, and Confidence*. New York: Harmony, 2016.

Jaworksi, Margaret. "The Negativity Bias: Why the Bad Stuff Sticks." Last updated February 19, 2020. https://www.psycom.net /negativity-bias.

Kamphoff, Cindra, and BJ Hellyer. "316: Managing Your Energy & Focus with BJ Hellyer, Fortune 100 Company Executive." *High Performance Mindset.* Podcast, uploaded March 7, 2020. https:// thehighperformancemindset.com/316-managing-your-energy-focus-with-bj-hellyer-managing-partner.

Manz, Charles C., Dennis Adsit, Sam Campbell, Margie Mathison-Hance. "Managerial Thought Patterns and Performance: A Study of Perceptual Patterns of Performance Hindrances for Higher and Lower Performing Managers." *Human Relations* 41, no. 6 (1988): 447–65. https://doi.org/10.1177/001872678804100603.

Neck, Christopher P., and Charles C. Manz. "Thought Self-Leadership: The Impact of Mental Strategies Training on Employee Cognition, Behavior, and Affect." *Journal of Organizational Behavior* 17, no. 5 (1996): 445–67. https://doi.org/10.1002/(SICI)10991379(199609)17:5 <445::AID-JOB770>3.0.CO;2-N.

Rogelberg, Steven G., Logan Justice, Phillip W. Braddy, Samantha C. Paustian-Underdahl, Eric Heggestad, Linda Shanock, Benjamin E. Baran, Tammy Beck, Shawn Long, Ashely Andrew, David G. Altman, and John W. Fleenor. "The Executive Mind: Leader Self-Talk, Effectiveness and Strain." *Journal of Managerial Psychology* 28, no. 2 (2013): 183–201. https://doi.org/10.1108/02683941311300702.

Sehgal, Kabir, and Deepak Chopra. "The Surprising Benefits of Journaling for 15 Minutes a Day—and 7 Prompts to Get You Started ." CNBC, July 25, 2019: https://www.cnbc.com /2019/07/25/deepak-chopra-benefits-of-journaling-and-8 -prompts-to-get-you-started.html.

Seligman, Martin. *Learned Optimism: How to Change Your Mind and Your Life.* New York: Random House, 2006.

Chapter 4

Bradberry, Travis, and Jean Greaves. *Emotional Intelligence* 2.0. San Diego: TalentSmart, 2009.

Covey, Stephen R. *The 8th Habit: From Effectiveness to Greatness.* New York: Simon & Schuster, 2004.

Csikszentmihalyi, Mihaly. *Flow: The Psychology of Optimal Experience.* New York: Harper Collins, 1990.

Eisenberger, Robert, Jason R. Jones, Florence Stinglhamber, Linda Shanock, and Amanda T. Randall. "Flow Experiences at Work: For ` Achievers Alone?" *Journal of Organizational Behavior* 26, no. 7 (2005): 755–75.

Eurich, Tasha. "What Self-Awareness Really Is (and How to Cultivate It)." *Harvard Business Review,* January 4, 2018. https://hbr.org/2018/01 /what-self-awareness-really-is-and-how-to-cultivate-it.

Frankl, Viktor. *Man's Search for Meaning.* Boston: Beacon Press, 2006.

Goleman, Daniel. *Emotional Intelligence: Why It Can Matter More than IQ.* New York: Bantam, 2006.

Hanson, Rick. "Emotional Hijacking." Accessed August 1, 2021. https://www.rickhanson.net/emotional-hijacking/?highlight =emotional%20temperament.

Jackson, Sue, and Mihaly Csikszentmihalyi. *Flow in Sports: The Keys to Optimal Experiences and Performances.* Champaign, IL: Human Kinetics, 1999.

Kamphoff, Cindra, and Susan Jackson. "359: How to Experience Flow More Often with Dr. Sue Jackson, Sport Psychologist, Flow Researcher & Author." *High Performance Mindset.* Podcast, uploaded August 5, 2020. https://thehighperformancemindset.com/359 -how-to-experience-flow-more-often-with-dr-sue-jackson-sport -psychologist-flow-researcher-author.

Kotler, Steven. *The Rise of the Superman: Decoding the Science of Ultimate Human Performance.* New York: Houghlin Mifflin, 2014.

Maxwell, John C. *The 21 Irrefutable Laws of Leadership: Follow Them and People Will Follow You.* New York: Harper Collins, 2007.

"Self-Awareness: A Key to Better Leadership." *MIT Sloan Management Review*, May 7, 2012. https://sloanreview.mit.edu/article/self -awareness-a-key-to-better-leadership/.

Chapter 5

Canfield, Jack. *The Success Principles: How to Get from Where You Are to Where You Want to Be.* New York: Harper Collins, 2005.

Canfield, Jack, Brandon Hall, and Janet Switzer. *The Success Principles Workbook: An Action Plan for Getting from Where You Are to Where You Want to Be.* New York: William Morrow Paperbacks, 2020.

David, Susan. *Emotional Agility: Get Unstuck, Embrace Change, and Thrive in Work and Life.* New York: Avery, 2016.

Gould, Daniel, Diane Guinan, Christy Greenleaf, Russ Medbery, and Kirsten Peterson. "Factors Affecting Olympic Performance: Perceptions of Athletes and Coaches from More and Less Successful Teams." *The Sport Psychologist* 13, no. 4 (1999): 371–94. https://doi .org/10.1123/tsp.13.4.371.

Ruiz, Don Miguel, and Janet Mills. *The Four Agreements: A Practical Guide to Personal Freedom.* San Rafael, CA: Amber-Allen Publishing, 1997.

Chapter 6

Bradt, Steve. "Wandering Mind Not a Happy Mind." *The Harvard Gazette*, November 11, 2010. https://news.harvard.edu/gazette/story/2010/11 /wandering-mind-not-a-happy-mind/.

Hyland, Patrick K., R. Andrew Lee, and Maura J. Mills. "Mindfulness at Work: A New Approach to Improving Individual and Organizational Performance." *Industrial and Organizational Psychology* 8, no. 4 (2015): 576–602. https://doi.org/10.1017/iop.2015.41.

Kabat-Zinn, Jon. *Full Catastrophe Living: Using the Wisdom of Your Body and Mind to Face Stress, Pain, and Illness.* New York: Bantam Dell, 1990.

Killingsworth, Matthew A., and Daniel T. Gilbert. "A Wandering Mind Is an Unhappy Mind." *Science 330*, no. 6006 (2010): 932. https://doi .org/10.1126/science.1192439.

Levin, Marissa. "Why Google, Nike, and Apple Love Mindfulness Training, and How You Can Easily Love It Too." *Inc.*, June 12, 2017: https://www.inc.com/marissa-levin/why-google-nike-and-apple -love-mindfulness-training-and-how-you-can-easily-love-.html.

Mumford, George. *The Mindful Athlete: Secrets to Pure Performance.* Berkeley, CA: Parallax, 2015.

Weisinger, Hendrie, and J. P. Pawliw-Fry. *Performing Under Pressure: The Science of Doing Your Best When It Matters Most.* New York: Crown Publishing, 2015.

Chapter 7

Avey, James B., Larry W. Hughes, Steven M. Norman, and Kyle W. Luthans. "Using Positivity, Transformational Leadership and Empowerment to Combat Employee Negativity." *Leadership & Organization Development Journal* 29, no. 2 (2008): 110–26. https:// doi.org/10.1108/01437730810852470.

Crane, Fredrick G., and Erinn C. Crane. "Dispositional Optimism and Entrepreneurial Success." *The Psychologist-Manager Journal* 10, no. 1 (2007) 13–25. https://doi.org/10.1080/10887150709336610.

David, Susan. *Emotional Agility: Get Unstuck, Embrace Change, and Thrive in Work and Life.* New York: Avery, 2016.

David, Susan. "Recognizing Your Emotions as Data, Not Directives." LinkedIn, February 3, 2021. https://www.linkedin.com/pulse /recognizing-your-emotions-data-directives-susan-david-ph-d-.

David, Susan, and Christina Congleton. "Emotional Agility." *Harvard Business Review*, November 2013. https://hbr.org/2013/11 /emotional-agility.

Dholakia, Utpal. "When Adversity Strikes, Optimism Helps Us Get Through." *Psychology Today*, October 30, 2016. https://www. psychologytoday.com/us/blog/the-science-behind-behavior /201610/when-adversity-strikes-optimism-helps-us-get-through.

Emmons, Robert A. *Thanks!: How Practicing Gratitude Can Make You Happier*. Boston: Mariner Books, 2008.

Ferguson, Yuna L., and Kennon M. Sheldon. "Trying to Be Happier Really Can Work: Two Experimental Studies." *The Journal of Positive Psychology 8*, no. 1 (2013): 23–33. https://doi.org/10.1080/17439760.2012.747000.

Foster, Sandra L., and Jeffrey E. Auerbach. *Positive Psychology in Coaching: Applying Science to Executive and Personal Coaching*. Executive College Press, 2019. Kindle.

Fredrickson, Barbara. *Positivity: Top-Notch Research Reveals the 3-to-1 Ratio That Will Change Your Life*. New York: Random House, 2009.

Fredrickson, Barbara L., and Marcial F. Losada. "Positive Affect and the Complex Dynamics of Human Flourishing." *American Psychologist* 60, no. 7 (2005): 678–86. https://doi.org/10.1037/0003-066X.60.7.678.

Losada, Marcial, and Emily Heaphy. "The Role of Positivity and Connectivity in the Performance of Business Teams: A Nonlinear Dynamics Model." *American Behavioral Scientist* 47, no. 6 (2004): 740–65. https://doi.org/10.1177/0002764203260208.

Lyubomirsky, Sonja. *The How of Happiness: A New Approach to Getting the Life You Want*. New York: Penguin Books, 2008.

Mongrain, Myriam, and Tracy Anselmo-Matthews. "Do Positive Psychology Exercises Work? A Replication of Seligman et al." *Journal of Clinical Psychology* 68, no. 4 (2012): 382–89. https://doi.org/10.1002/jclp.21839.

Schwantes, Marcel. "Why Are Your Employees Quitting? The Reason Comes Down to 3 Words (and No, 'Money' Isn't One of Them)." *Inc.*, February 20, 2019. https://www.inc.com/marcel-schwantes/why-do-people-quit-their-jobs-exactly-heres-entire-reason-in-3-simple-words.html.

Seligman, Martin E. P., Tracy A. Steen, Nansook Park, and Christopher Peterson. "Positive Psychology Progress: Empirical Validation of Interventions." *American Psychologist* 60, no. 5 (2005): 410–21. https://doi.org/10.1037/0003-066X.60.5.410.

Waters, Lea. "Predicting Job Satisfaction: Contributions of Individual Gratitude and Institutionalized Gratitude." *Psychology* 3, no. 12A (2012): 1174–76. https://doi.org/10.4236/psych.2012.312A173.

Zenger, Jack, and Joseph Folkman. "The Ideal Praise-to-Criticism Ratio." *Harvard Business Review*, March 15, 2013. https://hbr .org/2013/03/the-ideal-praise-to-criticism.

Chapter 8

Brown, Brené. *Dare to Lead: Brave Work. Tough Conversations. Whole Hearts.* New York: Random House, 2018.

Brown, Brené. *Brené Brown: The Call to Courage.* Netflix. https://www.netflix.com/title/81010166.

Brown, Brené. *The Gifts of Imperfection: 10th Anniversary Edition.* New York: Random House, 2020.

Canfield, Jack. *The Success Principles: How to Get from Where You Are to Where You Want to Be.* New York: Harper Collins, 2005.

Chamine, Shirzad. *Positive Intelligence: Why Only 20% of Teams and Individuals Achieve Their True Potential and How You Can Achieve Yours.* Austin, TX: Greenleaf Book Group, 2012.

George, Bill. *Authentic Leadership: Rediscovering the Secrets of Creating Lasting Value.* San Francisco: Jossey-Bass, 2003.

George, Bill. *Discover Your True North: Becoming an Authentic Leader.* San Francisco: Jossey-Bass, 2015.

Kamphoff, Cindra, and Jack Canfield. "351: The Success Principles with Jack Canfield, America's #1 Success Coach & New York Times Bestseller." *High Performance Mindset.* Podcast, uploaded July 2, 2020. https://thehighperformancemindset.com/episode-351-the-success -principles-with-jack-canfield-americas-1-success-coach-new-york -times-bestseller.

Loehr, Jim. *The Power of Story: Rewrite Your Destiny in Business and in Life.* New York: Free Press, 2008.

Luft, Joseph, and Harry Ingham. *The Johari Window, a Graphic Model of Interpersonal Awareness*. Proceedings of the western training laboratory in group development. Los Angeles: University of California, Los Angeles, 1955.

Maslow, A. H. *A Theory of Human Motivation*. Eastford, CT: Martino Fine Books, 2013.

Maslow, A. H. "A Theory of Human Motivation." *Psychological Review* 50, no. 4 (1943). 370–96. https://doi.org/10.1037/h0054346.

Rego, Arménio, Filipa Sousa, Carla Marques, and Miguel Pina e Cunha. "Authentic Leadership Promoting Employees' Psychological Capital and Creativity." *Journal of Business Research* 65, no. 3 (2012): 429–37. https://doi.org/10.1016/j.jbusres.2011.10.003.

Chapter 9

Afremow, Jim. *The Champion's Mind: How Great Athletes Think, Train, and Thrive*. New York: Rodale, 2015.

Breines, Juliana G., and Serena Chen. "Self-Compassion Increases Self-Improvement Motivation." *Personality and Social Psychology Bulletin* 38, no. 9 (2012): 1133–43. https://doi.org/10.1177/0146167212445599.

Duhigg, Charles. "What Google Learned From Its Quest to Build a Perfect Team." *The New York Times Magazine*, February 25, 2016. https://www.nytimes.com/2016/02/28/magazine/what-google-learned-from-its-quest-to-build-the-perfect-team.html.

Edmondson, Amy. *The Fearless Organization: Creating Psychological Safety in the Workplace for Learning, Innovation, and Growth*. New York: Wiley, 2018.

Herway, Jake. "How to Create a Culture of Psychological Safety." *Gallup*, December 7, 2017. https://www.gallup.com/workplace/236198/create-culture-psychological-safety.aspx.

Morin, Amy. *13 Things Mentally Strong People Don't Do: Take Back Your Power, Embrace Change, Face Your Fears, and Train Your Brain for Happiness and Success*. New York: William Morrow, 2017.

Neff, Kristen. *Self-Compassion: The Proven Power of Being Kind to Yourself.* New York: William Morrow, 2010.

Schwantes, Marcel. "Why Are Your Employees Quitting? The Reason Comes Down to 3 Words (and No, 'Money' Isn't One of Them)." *Inc.*, February 20, 2019. https://www.inc.com/marcel-schwantes/why-do-people-quit-their-jobs-exactly-heres-entire-reason-in-3-simple-words.html.

Stein, Alan, Jr., and Jon Sternfeld. *Raise Your Game: High-Performance Secrets from the Best of the Best.* New York: Center Street, 2020.

"Understand Team Effectiveness." re:Work. Google. Accessed August 23, 2021. https://rework.withgoogle.com/print/guides/5721312655835136/.

Vaisman, Josh. "The Solutions to Your Problems Lie Within." *Flourish Veterinary Consulting,* July 5, 2018. https://www.flourishveterinaryconsulting.com/post/the-solutions-to-your-problems-lie-within.

Chapter 10

Branson, Richard. *Finding My Virginity: The New Autobiography.* New York: Portfolio, 2017.

Coleman, Alison. "How Entrepreneurs Like Richard Branson Handle Business Risk." *Forbes*, December 21, 2018. https://www.forbes.com/sites/alisoncoleman/2018/12/21/how-entrepreneurs-like-richard-branson-handle-business-risk/?sh=56f255ac462b.

Fogg, BJ. *Tiny Habits: The Small Changes That Change Everything.* Boston: Mariner Books, 2021.

Kamphoff, Cindra, and Shannon Polson. "355: The Grit Factor with Shannon Huffman Polson, Speaker, Author and CEO of The Grit Institute." *High Performance Mindset.* Podcast, uploaded July 16, 2020. https://www.cindrakamphoff.com/shannon/.

Maxwell, John C. *21 Irrefutable Laws of Leadership: Follow Them and People Will Follow You.* New York: Harper Collins Leadership, 2007.

Maxwell, John C. *How Successful People Think: Change Your Thinking, Change Your Life.* New York: Center Street, 2009.

McGonigal, Kelly. *The Upside of Stress: Why Stress Is Good for You, and How to Get Good at It.* New York: Avery, 2016.

Partners in Leadership. "5 Wildly Successful Entrepreneurs Reveal How Risk Taking Propelled Their Careers." *Inc.*, October 3, 2018. https://www.inc.com/partners-in-leadership/5-wildly-successful -entrepreneurs-reveal-how-risk-taking-propelled-their-careers.html.

Phelps, David. "From Cows to Quartz, Davis Family Cuts a Wide Business Swath." *Star Tribune*, December 18, 2014. https:// www.startribune.com/no-14-under-the-radar-st-peter-family -among-richest-americans/284917381/.

Warner, Jennifer. "Are Risk Takers Happier? Taking Risks Tied to Age, Height, and Happiness." *WebMD*, September 19, 2005. https:// www.webmd.com/balance/news/20050919/are-risk-takers-happier.